VIRGINIA

GO MATH!

| Middle School | Grade 6 |

STANDARDS OF LEARNING *SUCCESS*

Edward B. Burger • Juli K. Dixon
Timothy D. Kanold • Matthew R. Larson
Steven J. Leinwand • Martha E. Sandoval-Martinez

Grade 6 VA SOL Success Lessons

Table of Contents

Adding Integers with the Same Sign

? ESSENTIAL QUESTION

How do you add integers with the same sign?

EXPLORE ACTIVITY 1

Modeling Sums of Integers with the Same Sign

Colored counters can be used to add positive integers and to add negative integers.

○ = +1
● = −1

Model with two-color counters.

A $2 + 4$

2 positive counters   ○○

4 positive counters   ○○○○ } total number of counters

How many counters are there in total? _____

What is the sum? How did you find it?

_____

_____

B $-3 + (-1)$

3 negative counters   ●●●

1 negative counter   ● } total number of counters

How many counters are there in total? _____

Notice that the counters are negative. What is the sum? _____

Reflect

1. **Make a Conjecture** If you add two integers with the same sign, what do you know about the sign of the sum?

_____

_____

Adding on a Number Line

Positive and negative numbers can be represented on a number line. For example, the arrow shown is for 3. The arrow is 3 units long and points in the positive direction. An arrow for –3 would be 3 units long and point in the negative direction.

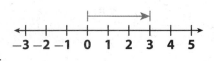

Kate owes her mother $5. She borrows another $3. What is the total amount she owes her mother, written as an integer?

A Represent the initial amount she owes her mother as an integer.

_____

B Draw the arrow on the number line for the initial amount she owes.

C Borrowing another $3 is like adding –$3 to the amount she already owes. To add –3, start at the tip of your first arrow, and draw an arrow representing –3. A single arrow from the start of your first arrow to the end of your second arrow represents the sum.

D Represent the total amount Kate owes her mother, written as an integer.

_____

Reflect

2. What If? Suppose Kate owed her mother $4 and borrowed another $2. Explain how to use the number line to find the integer representing the total she owes her mother.

_____

_____

_____

3. Communicate Mathematical Ideas How is using a horizontal number line to add two negative integers different from using a horizontal number line to add two positive integers?

_____

_____

_____

_____

4. Critical Thinking What are two negative integers that have a sum of −10?

_____

Adding Integers with a Common Sign

Another way to add integers with the same sign is by adding the absolute value of the integers and using the sign of the integers for the sum.

EXAMPLE

Add −8 + (−9).   The signs of both integers are the same.

STEP 1 $|-8| = 8$ Find the absolute values.

$|-9| = 9$ The absolute value is always positive or zero.

STEP 2 Find the sum of the absolute values

$8 + 9 = 17$.

STEP 3 Use the sign of the integers for the sum.

$-8 + (-9) = -17$ Both integers are negative.

Reflect

5. **What If?** Find the sum −9 + (−8). Does changing the order in which you add two negative integers change the sum? Explain.

_____

_____

_____

_____

6. **Communicate Mathematical Ideas** Can you use the method shown in the Example to find the sum of two positive integers? Give an example.

_____

_____

_____

_____

7. How does using absolute value compare to using a number line to add integers with the same sign?

_____

_____

_____

_____

_____

Find each sum.

1. $-4 + (-3)$

   a. How many counters are there? _____

   b. Do the counters represent positive or

      negative integers? _____

   c. $-4 + (-3) = $ _____

2. $-6 + (-5)$

   a. How many counters are there? _____

   b. Do the counters represent positive or

      negative integers? _____

   c. $-6 + (-5) = $ _____

Model each addition problem on the number line to find the sum.

3. $-4 + (-4) = $ _____

4. $-1 + (-5) = $ _____

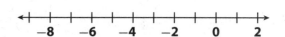

5. $-4 + (-8) = $ _____

6. $-3 + (-7) = $ _____

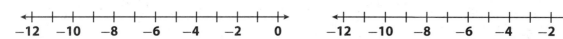

Find each sum.

7. $-2 + (-9) = $ _____

8. $-1 + (-8) = $ _____

9. $-11 + (-3) = $ _____

10. $-9 + (-9) = $ _____

11. For the first round of mini golf, Paul's final score was −1. His score for the second round was −2. What was Paul's total score for the two rounds?

_____

12. The temperature was 6°F below zero. The temperature drops by 4°F. Write and evaluate a sum to find the new temperature.

_____

13. Jamie withdrew $15 and $10 from her checking account. Write and evaluate a sum to show the total change in the value of her account.

_____

Adding Integers with Different Signs

ESSENTIAL QUESTION

How do you add integers with different signs?

EXPLORE ACTIVITY 1

Adding on a Number Line

When you add integers with different signs on a number line, one of the arrows "cancels out" at least part of the other. What remains is the sum.

The 2 units remaining on the arrow pointing right show that the sum is 2.

The 2 units remaining on the arrow pointing left show that the sum is -2.

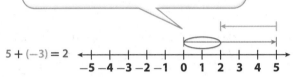

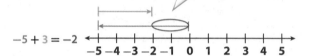

Model each sum on a number line.

A Model $6 + (-3)$.

Start at 0. Draw the arrow for 6. Then, starting directly above the tip of the arrow for 6, draw the arrow for -3.

$6 + (-3) =$ _____

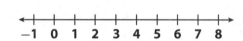

B Model $-3 + 2$.

Start at _____. Draw the arrow for _____.

Then, starting at _____, draw the arrow for _____.

$-3 + 2 =$ _____

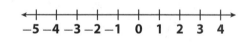

C Model $7 + (-7)$.

Start at _____. Draw the arrow for _____.

Then, starting at _____, draw the arrow for _____.

$7 + (-7) =$ _____

Reflect

1. **Make a Prediction** You add a negative and a positive integer. The absolute value of the negative integer is greater than the absolute value of the positive integer. Will the sum be positive or negative?

_____

_____

_____

Modeling Sums of Integers with Different Signs

Colored counters can be used to add integers with different signs. When you add +1 (one yellow counter) and −1 (one red counter), the result is 0. One red and one yellow counter form a *zero pair*.

$1 + (-1) = 0$

Model and find each sum using counters. Part A is done for you. For Part B, follow the steps to model and find the sum using counters.

A Model $4 + (-3)$.

Start with 4 positive counters to represent 4.

Add 3 negative counters to represent adding −3.

Form zero pairs.

What is left when you remove the zero pairs?

_____ counter(s)

Find the sum: $4 + (-3) =$ _____

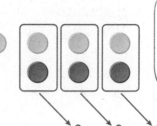

> The value of a zero pair is 0. Adding 0 to any number does not change its value.

0   0   0

B Model $-8 + 5$.

Start with _____ counters to represent _____.

Add _____ counters to represent adding _____.

Form zero pairs.

What is left when you remove the zero pairs?

_____ counter(s)

Find the sum: $-8 + 5 =$ _____

Reflect

2. **Make a Prediction** Simone models a sum using counters. She uses fewer negative (red) counters than positive (yellow) counters. Will the sum be positive or negative? Explain.

_____

_____

Adding Integers

You know how to add integers with the same sign and how to add integers with different signs. The table summarizes the rules for adding integers.

	Adding Integers	Examples
Same signs	Add the absolute values of the integers. Use the common sign for the sum.	$7 + 6 = 13$ $-4 + (-8) = -12$
Different signs	Subtract the lesser absolute value from the greater absolute value. Use the sign of the integer with the greater absolute value for the sum.	$5 + (-10) = -5$ $-5 + 2 = -3$
A number and its opposite	The sum is 0. The opposite of any number is called its **additive inverse**.	$6 + (-6) = 0$ $-12 + 12 = 0$

EXAMPLE

Find each sum.

A $-9 + 5$

$|-9| - |5| = 4$ Subtract the lesser absolute value from the greater.

$-9 + 5 = -4$ Use the sign of the number with the greater absolute value.

B $24 + (-24)$

$24 + (-24) = 0$ The sum of a number and its opposite is 0.

Reflect

3. Make a Prediction Will the sum of 25 and -34 be a positive or negative number? Explain how you know.

_____

_____

_____

4. Communicate Mathematical Ideas How does adding $9 + (-5)$ compare to adding $-9 + 5$?

_____

_____

_____

_____

_____

Use a number line to find each sum.

1. $-4 + 7 =$ _____

2. $3 + (-5) =$ _____

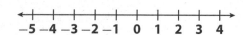

Circle the zero pairs in each model. Find the sum.

3. $-2 + 3 =$ _____

4. $4 + (-6) =$ _____

Find each sum.

5. $-7 + 15 =$ _____

6. $9 + (-6) =$ _____

7. $8 + (-16) =$ _____

8. $-17 + 21 =$ _____

9. $-13 + 12 =$ _____

10. $24 + (-10) =$ _____

11. The temperature was 2 °F below zero. The temperature rose by 8 °F. What is the temperature now?

_____

12. Lynn had a checking account balance of $25. Then she withdrew $10. What is the new balance of Lynn's checking account?

_____

13. A football team lost 15 yards on the first play and then on the next play they gained 15 yards. What was the overall change in field position?

_____

14. **Critical Thinking** Suppose the sum of 2 and another integer is a negative integer. What can you conclude about the other integer? Explain.

_____

_____

_____

15. **Analyze Relationships** When adding integers with different signs, does the order in which you add the integers matter? Explain.

_____

_____

_____

LESSON S.3 Subtracting Integers

ESSENTIAL QUESTION

How do you subtract integers?

EXPLORE ACTIVITY 1

Modeling Integer Subtraction

You can use counters to find the difference of two integers. In some cases, you may need to add zero pairs.

$1 + (-1) = 0$

Model and find each difference using counters.

A Model $-5 - (-2)$.

Start with 5 negative counters to represent -5.

Take away 2 negative counters to represent subtracting -2.

What is left? _____

Find the difference: $-5 - (-2) =$ _____

B Model $8 - (-4)$.

Start with 8 positive counters to represent 8.

You need to take away 4 negative counters, so add 4 zero pairs.

Take away 4 negative counters to represent subtracting -4.

What is left? _____

Find the difference: $8 - (-4) =$ _____

C Model $-4 - 3$.

Start with _____ counters.

You need to take away _____ counters, so add _____ zero pairs.

Take away _____ counters.

What is left? _____

Find the difference: $-4 - 3 =$ _____

Reflect

1. **Communicate Mathematical Ideas** Suppose you want to model the difference 5 − 7. Do you need to add zero pairs? If so, how many should you add? Explain. What is the difference?

_____

_____

_____

Subtracting on a Number Line

To model the difference 4 − 2 on a number line, you start at 0 and move 4 units to the right, then move 2 units to the left. Notice that you model the sum 4 + (−2) in the same way. Subtracting 2 is the same as adding its opposite, −2.

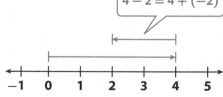

You can use the fact that subtracting a number is the same as adding its opposite to find a difference of two integers.

Find each difference on a number line.

A Find −2 − 3 on a number line.

Rewrite subtraction as addition of the opposite.

−2 − 3 = −2 + _____

Start at _____. Draw the arrow for _____.

Then, starting at _____, draw the arrow for _____.

The difference is _____.

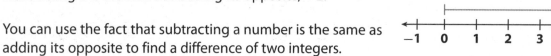

B Find −6 − (−4) on a number line.

Rewrite subtraction as addition of the opposite.

−6 − (−4) = −6 + _____

Start at _____. Draw the arrow for _____.

Then, starting at _____, draw the arrow for _____.

The difference is _____.

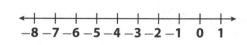

Subtracting Integers by Adding the Opposite

You can use the fact that subtracting an integer is the same as adding its opposite to solve problems.

EXAMPLE

A **After the first day of a golf tournament, Sonny's golf score was −4. His final score was −1. Find the change in his score.**

STEP 1 Write a subtraction expression.

final score − first day's score = change in score

$-1 - (-4)$

STEP 2 Find the difference.

$-1 - (-4) = -1 + 4$ To subtract −4, add its opposite, 4.

$-1 + 4 = 3$ Use the rule for adding integers.

His score increased by 3.

B **The temperature in the afternoon was 40 °F. By midnight, the temperature was 25 °F. Find the change in temperature.**

STEP 1 Write a subtraction expression.

final temperature − starting temperature = change in temperature

$25 - 40$

STEP 2 Find the difference.

$25 - 40 = 25 + (-40)$ To subtract 40, add its opposite, −40.

$25 + (-40) = -15$ Use the rule for adding integers.

The temperature decreased by 15 °F.

Reflect

3. **What If?** In Part A, Sonny's final score was −1. Suppose his final score was −6. Predict whether the change in his score was positive or negative. Then subtract to find the change.

_____.

Explain how to find each difference using counters.

1. $-8 - (-5) = $ _____

_____

_____

_____

_____

2. $5 - (-2) = $ _____

_____

_____

_____

_____

Use a number line to find each difference.

3. $-3 - 5 = -3 + $ _____ $ = $ _____

4. $-10 - (-4) = -10 + $ _____ $ = $ _____

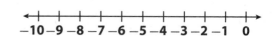

Find each difference.

5. $6 - 12 = $ _____

6. $-2 - (-7) = $ _____

7. $10 - 14 = $ _____

8. $-13 - 2 = $ _____

9. $0 - (-1) = $ _____

10. $-7 - (-21) = $ _____

Find the difference. Write the subtraction expression and rewrite it as addition of the opposite.

11. The temperature was -9 °F this morning. By afternoon, the temperature was -4 °F. What is the change in temperature?

_____

12. At the start of the day, Natalie's checking account balance was $-\$25$. By the end of the day, it was $5. What is the change in her account balance?

_____

13. George is playing a video game. His score at the start of the game was -15 points. By the end of the game it was -55 points. What is the change in George's score?

_____

14. Critical Thinking When subtracting integers, does the order in which you subtract the integers matter? Explain.

_____

_____

LESSON S.4 Multiplying Integers

How do you multiply integers?

EXPLORE ACTIVITY 1

Multiplying Integers Using a Number Line

You can use a number line to see what happens when you multiply a positive number by a negative number.

A For two consecutive hours, the temperature dropped 4 °F. What was the change in temperature?

Find 2(−4).

To graph −4, you would start at 0 and move _____ units to the left.

2(−4) means (_____) + (_____).

To graph 2(−4), start at 0 and move _____ units to the left _____ times.

The result is _____.

The change in temperature was _____.

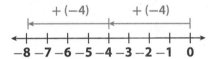

B Simon carried the football 4 times in a row. Each time he lost 2 yards. What was the change in yardage?

Find 4(−2).

4(−2) means (_____) + (_____) + (_____) + (_____).

Show this on the number line.

The total change in yardage was _____.

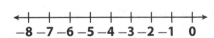

Reflect

1. **What if?** Suppose the temperature dropped 4 °F for three consecutive hours. What would be the change in temperature? Explain your reasoning.

_____

_____

Modeling Integer Multiplication

Counters representing positive and negative numbers can help you understand how to find the product of two negative integers.

Find the product of −2 and −5.

Write (−2)(−5) as −2(−5), which means the *opposite* of 2(−5).

STEP 1 Use negative counters to model 2(−5).

2 groups of −5

STEP 2 Make the same model using positive counters to find the *opposite* of 2(−5).

the *opposite* of 2 groups of −5

STEP 3 Translate the model into a mathematical expression:

(−2)(−5) = _____

The product of −2 and −5 is _____.

Reflect

2. **What If?** Is the product of −4 and −5 positive or negative? Explain.

    _____

    _____

    _____

    _____

3. **Make a Conjecture** Is the product of two negative integers positive or negative? What about the product of two positive integers? What can you conclude about the product of any two integers with the same sign?

    _____

    _____

Multiplying Integers

The product of two integers with opposite signs is negative. The product of two integers with the same sign is positive. The product of 0 and any other integer is 0.

EXAMPLE

A Find $(11)(-4)$.

STEP 1 Determine the sign of the product.

11 is positive and −4 is negative. Since the numbers have opposite signs, the product will be negative.

STEP 2 Find the absolute values of the numbers and multiply them.

$|11| = 11 \quad |-4| = 4$

$11 \times 4 = 44$

STEP 3 Assign the correct sign to the product.

$11(-4) = -44$ The product is −44.

B Find $(-7)(-9)$.

STEP 1 Determine the sign of the product.

−7 is negative and −9 is negative. Since the numbers have the same sign, the product will be positive.

STEP 2 Find the absolute values of the numbers and multiply them.

$|-7| = 7 \quad\quad |-9| = 9$

$7 \times 9 = 63$

STEP 3 Assign the correct sign to the product.

$(-7)(-9) = 63$ The product is 63.

C Find $(-20)(0)$.

$(-20)(0) = 0$ One of the factors is 0, so the product is 0.

Use a number line to find each product.

1. $3(-3) = $ _____

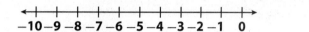

2. $2(-5) = $ _____

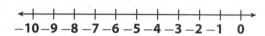

Explain how to find each product using counters.

3. $-3(-6)$

_____

_____

_____

_____

_____

_____

4. $-4(-4)$

_____

_____

_____

_____

_____

_____

Find each product.

5. $-7(1)$ _____

6. $10(-2)$ _____

7. $-5(-5)$ _____

8. $-6(-11)$ _____

9. $-4(9)$ _____

10. $-8(8)$ _____

11. $(-5)(10)$ _____

12. $-4(25)$ _____

13. $-3(-30)$ _____

14. Jace is playing a trivia game. Each time he answers a question incorrectly he loses 5 points. Jace answers 3 questions incorrectly in a row. If he started with 0 points, what is Jace's score now?

_____

15. Amy made 2 withdrawals of $20 from her checking account. What was the change in the amount in her checking account?

_____

16. Charles is scuba diving. He descends 6 feet below sea level. He descends the same distance 3 more times. What is Charles's final elevation?

_____

17. **Critical Thinking** The product of two integers is −20. Identify two sets of possible factors.

_____

LESSON
S.5 Dividing Integers

How do you divide integers?

EXPLORE ACTIVITY

Dividing Integers Using a Number Line

A climber is descending 90 feet into a canyon. He wants to do it in 3 equal descents. How far should he travel in each descent?

A Use the number line to find how far the climber should travel in each of the 3 descents.

B To solve this problem, set up a division problem: $\dfrac{-90}{\square} = ?$

C Rewrite the division problem as a multiplication problem.

_____ × ? = −90

D Remember the rules for integer multiplication. If the product is negative, one of the factors must be negative. Since _____ is positive, the unknown factor must be _____.

E You know that 3 × _____ = 90. So, using the rules for integer multiplication, you can say that 3 × _____ = −90.

The climber should descend _____ feet in each descent.

F Use the process you just learned to find each of the quotients below.

$\dfrac{-20}{5} = \square$ $\dfrac{-42}{-7} = \square$ $\dfrac{44}{-4} = \square$ $\dfrac{-24}{8} = \square$

```
 0 ─┼─
-10 ─┼─
-20 ─┼─
-30 ─┼─
-40 ─┼─
-50 ─┼─
-60 ─┼─
-70 ─┼─
-80 ─┼─
-90 ─┼─
-100 ─┼─
```

Reflect

1. **What If?** A climber wants to make the descent in 5 equal descents. How far should he travel in each descent? How does this compare to doing the descent in 3 equal descents? Explain.

_____

_____

Dividing Integers

You used the relationship between multiplication and division to make conjectures about the signs of quotients of integers.

You can also use multiplication to understand why division by zero is not possible. Think about the division problem below and its related multiplication problem.

$$10 \div 0 = ? \qquad\qquad 0 \times ? = 10$$

The multiplication sentence says that there is some number times 0 that equals 10. You already know that 0 times any number equals 0. This means that division by 0 is not possible, so we say that division by 0 is *undefined*.

EXAMPLE 1

A **Divide: $30 \div (-5)$**

STEP 1 Determine the sign of the quotient.

30 is positive and −5 is negative. Since the numbers have opposite signs, the quotient will be negative.

STEP 2 Divide.

$$30 \div (-5) = -6$$

B **Divide: $-18 \div (-9)$**

STEP 1 Determine the sign of the quotient.

−18 is negative and −9 is negative. Since the numbers have the same sign, the quotient will be positive.

STEP 2 Divide.

$$-18 \div (-9) = 2$$

C **Divide: $0 \div (-3)$**

STEP 1 Determine the sign of the quotient.

The dividend is 0 and the divisor is not 0. So, the quotient is 0.

> While a number divided by 0 is undefined, 0 divided by a number will always be 0.

STEP 2 Divide.

$$0 \div (-3) = 0$$

Reflect

2. **Analyze Relationships** Compare the quotient of −35 divided by 5 to the quotient of 35 divided by −5. How are the division statements similar?

_____

_____

_____

Using Integer Division to Solve Problems

As seen in the Explore Activity, you can use integer division to solve real-world problems. For some problems, you may need to perform more than one step. Be sure to check that the sign of the quotient makes sense for the situation.

EXAMPLE 2

Jodi's fantasy baseball league has the settings shown below for pitchers.

Pitcher's Stat Category	Points
Innings	1
Wins	10
Losses	−7
Complete Games	5
Shutouts	5
Saves	7
Blown Saves	−3
Hits	−0.5

Jodi's pitchers have a total of −35 points from losses and −18 points from blown saves. Which has occurred more times?

STEP 1 Find the number of losses Jodi's pitchers have.

$-35 \div (-7) = 5$ *Divide the total points for losses by the points for each loss.*

STEP 2 Find the number of blown saves Jodi's pitchers have.

$-18 \div (-3) = 6$ *Divide the total score for blown saves by the score for each blown save.*

STEP 3 Compare the number of each.

$6 > 5$, so Jodi's pitchers have more blown saves than losses.

Reflect

4. **Communicate Mathematical Ideas** What expressions can you use to check your answers to Steps 1 and 2 above? Evaluate each expression. What do the results represent?

_____

_____

_____

Practice

Use a number line to find each quotient.

1. $-8 \div 4 =$ _____

2. $-12 \div 3 =$ _____

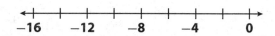

Find each quotient.

3. $\dfrac{-24}{8}$ _____

4. $\dfrac{-36}{-9}$ _____

5. $-18 \div 6$ _____

6. $28 \div (-14)$ _____

7. $21 \div (-3)$ _____

8. $\dfrac{25}{5}$ _____

9. $-10 \div 1$ _____

10. $\dfrac{0}{-1}$ _____

11. $\dfrac{-144}{-12}$ _____

12. $-100 \div 20$ _____

13. $-66 \div (-3)$ _____

14. $\dfrac{-2}{0}$ _____

Write a division expression for each problem. Then find the value of the expression.

15. Mei's score in a video game changed by -26 points because she answered questions incorrectly. Her score changed -2 points for each missed question. How many questions did Mei miss?

_____

16. Kenny is charged each time he uses the swimming pool. His bank account changes by $-\$4$ each time. If his account has a change of $-\$52$ during the summer months, how many times did Kenny go swimming during the summer? _____

17. A scuba diver needs to descend to a depth of 150 feet. He wants to do it in 6 equal descents. How far should he travel in each descent? _____

18. Chloe made 3 of her credit card payments late and was charged 3 late fees. The total change in her account balance was $-\$72$. What was the change in her account for each late fee?

_____

19. **Critical Thinking** Write two different division problems whose quotient is -5.

_____

20. **Communicate Mathematical Ideas** How is the process of dividing two integers similar to the process of multiplying two integers?

_____

_____

Applying Integer Operations

? ESSENTIAL QUESTION

How can you use integer operations to solve real-world problems?

EXPLORE ACTIVITY

Using the Order of Operations with Integers

The **order of operations** applies to integer operations as well as to positive number operations. Perform multiplication and division first, then addition and subtraction. Work from left to right in the expression.

Devin has a checking account with a debit card. He used his debit card to make three $40 cash withdrawals from his account and then a $125 purchase at a store. What is the change in his checking account?

Analyze Information

You need to find the total *change* in Devin's checking account. Since using a debit card causes a *decrease* in the amount in the account, use negative integers to represent these amounts.

Formulate a Plan

Write an expression that shows the total change in the balance.

Write a product to represent the three cash withdrawals.

$$-40 + (-40) + (-40) = 3\left(\boxed{}\right)$$

Add -125 to represent the store purchase.

$$3\left(\boxed{}\right) + \left(\boxed{}\right)$$

Solve

Evaluate the expression to find by how much the amount in the account changed.

Multiply first. Then add.

$$3(-40) + (-125) = \boxed{} + (-125) = \boxed{}$$

The amount in the account **increased / decreased** by $ _____ .

Justify and Evaluate

The value -245 represents a *decrease* of $245. This makes sense since withdrawals and debit card purchases remove money from a checking account.

Reflect

1. **What If?** Suppose Devin made three $40 withdrawals and one $125 deposit. Write and evaluate an expression that represents the situation. What is the change in his account?

Using Negative Integers to Represent Quantities

You can use positive and negative integers to solve problems involving amounts that increase or decrease. Sometimes you may need to use more than one operation.

EXAMPLE 1

Six friends go out to lunch together. The total cost of lunch is $60, and the six friends split the cost evenly. Amy uses her debit card to pay her share and also includes a $2 tip. What is the change in Amy's checking account balance after she pays for her dinner?

STEP 1 Determine the signs of the values and the operations you will use. Then write an expression.

A debit card purchase removes money from an account, so it will *decrease* the amount of money in the account. Use the negative integers –60 and –2 for the debit. Use the positive integer 6 for the six friends.

> The cost is *split evenly*. Divide to find 6 equal parts of –60.

> Add the tip.

Change to Amy's checking account: $(-60) \div 6 + (-2)$

STEP 2 Evaluate the expression.

$$(-60) \div 6 + (-2) = -10 + (-2) \qquad \text{Divide.}$$
$$= -12 \qquad \text{Add.}$$

The balance in Amy's account will decrease by $12.

Reflect

2. **What If?** Suppose there were 4 friends in Example 1. How much would be debited from Amy's account if the tip remained the same? Show your work.

Comparing Values of Expressions

Some problem situations require comparing two values. Use integer operations to calculate values. Then compare the values.

EXAMPLE 2

Ravi and Elena are playing a game in which they move a game piece along a number line. They both start at zero. Ravi moves forward 2 units, then back 3 units 3 times. Elena moves forward 4 units, then back 4 units 2 times. Find each player's change in position. Which player is closer to zero now?

STEP 1   Write an expression to represent each player's situation.

Ravi: $2 + 3(-3)$

Elena: $4 + 2(-4)$

STEP 2   Evaluate the expressions to find each player's overall change in position.

Ravi: $2 + 3(-3) = 2 + (-9)$ Multiply.

$= -7$ Add.

Ravi's position is –7, or 7 units to the left of zero.

Elena: $4 + 2(-4) = 4 + (-8)$ Multiply.

$= -4$ Add.

Elena's position is –4, or 4 units to the left of zero.

> Remember, *absolute value* is the distance of a number from zero on a number line. Absolute value is always positive. $|-2| = 2$

STEP 3   Use absolute value to compare the two players' positions.

$|-7| > |-4|$ Compare absolute values.

Elena's position is 4 units away from zero, so she is closer to zero than Ravi's.

Reflect

3. **What If?** Suppose Ravi moves *back* 2 units 1 time, then *forward* 3 units 3 times. Would Ravi's change in position be the same or different? Explain.

_____

_____

_____

Evaluate each expression.

1. $2(-5) - 4$ _____

2. $7 + (-24) \div (-6)$ _____

3. $15 + (-15) \div 3$ _____

4. $-4(8) + 11$ _____

5. $-42 \div (-6) - 14$ _____

6. $-9 + (-9)(0)$ _____

Write an expression to represent the situation. Evaluate the expression and answer the question.

7. Ryan buys 4 T-shirts for $12 each. He also returns an $18 dress shirt. What is the total change to the amount of money he has?

_____

8. Elizabeth took a math quiz. She lost 2 points each for 7 incorrect answers. She earned 5 points for answering a bonus question correctly. How many points did Elizabeth lose or receive overall?

_____

9. Alicia is playing a game on her computer. She starts out with 100 points but loses 15 points 8 times. Then she loses 20 points for an illegal move. What is the total change to her score?

_____

10. Wilson has an account at an app store. He buys 5 new apps for his smartphone at $3 each. Then he receives a $20 credit for being a loyal customer. By how much does the amount in his account change?

_____

Compare the values of the two expressions using $<$, $=$, or $>$.

11. $-2(-4) + 3$ _____ $5(-4) + 11$

12. $-12 + (-3)(-2)$ _____ $4(-2) + 2$

13. $-14 \div 2 - 8$ _____ $-2(-3) + 1$

14. $|-8(2) - 3|$ _____ $|-7(3) - 1|$

15. Critique Reasoning Nicki found the quotient of two integers and got a negative integer. She added another integer to the quotient and got a negative integer. Her brother says that all the integers Nicki used must be negative. Do you agree? Explain.

_____

_____

_____

Modeling Multiplying Fractions

? ESSENTIAL QUESTION How do you model multiplication of fractions and mixed numbers?

EXPLORE ACTIVITY 1

Modeling Fraction Multiplication

You can model the multiplication of fractions in different ways. One way is to use an *area model*.

Jasmine has $\frac{1}{2}$ pint of soy milk. She uses $\frac{3}{4}$ of it to make a smoothie. How much soy milk does she use for the smoothie?

To find $\frac{3}{4}$ of $\frac{1}{2}$, model the expression $\frac{3}{4} \cdot \frac{1}{2}$ on a grid.

A First, model $\frac{1}{2}$ to represent $\frac{1}{2}$ pint of soy milk.

The denominator of the fraction is 2, so the grid is divided vertically into 2 equal parts.

The numerator is 1, so shade the first vertical part.

B Next, model $\frac{3}{4}$ to represent the fraction that Jasmine used.

The denominator is 4, so the grid is divided horizontally into 4 equal parts.

The numerator is 3. Use a different color to shade the first 3 horizontal parts.

C The area where the two colors overlap represents $\frac{3}{4}$ of $\frac{1}{2}$ pint.

The grid is divided into a total of _____ equal parts.

The two colors overlap in _____ of the equal parts.

$\dfrac{3}{4} \cdot \dfrac{1}{2} = \dfrac{\bigcirc}{\bigcirc}$ ← total number of overlapping parts
← number of parts in one grid

Jasmine used _____ pint of soy milk in the smoothie.

Reflect

1. **Communicate Mathematical Ideas** Explain how the number of columns and the number of rows in the grid are related to the denominator of the fraction in your answer.

_____

_____

Modeling Multiplication of a Fraction and Mixed Number

You also can use an area model to show the multiplication of a fraction and a mixed number.

Oliver will run $1\frac{1}{4}$ miles during track practice. So far, he has run $\frac{2}{3}$ of this distance. The expression $\frac{2}{3} \cdot 1\frac{1}{4}$ to find the distance, in miles, that Oliver has already run. Use the grids to model the multiplication.

A First, model $1\frac{1}{4}$ to represent $1\frac{1}{4}$ miles.

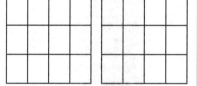

The denominator of the fraction is 4, so each grid is divided vertically into 4 equal parts.

Shade 1 whole grid to represent the whole number 1. Shade the first vertical part of the second grid to represent the fraction $\frac{1}{4}$.

B Next, model $\frac{2}{3}$ to represent the fraction of the distance Oliver has run.

The denominator is 3, so each grid is divided horizontally into 3 equal parts.

The numerator is 2. Use a different color to shade the first two horizontal parts of each grid.

C The area where the two colors overlap represents $\frac{2}{3}$ of $1\frac{1}{4}$ miles, or the distance Oliver has run so far.

Each grid is divided into a total of _____ parts.

The total number of parts where the two colors overlap is _____.

$\frac{2}{3} \cdot \frac{5}{4} = \dfrac{\bigcirc}{\bigcirc}$ ⟵ total number of overlapping parts

⟵ number of parts in one grid

So far, Oliver has run _____ mile, which simplifies to $\dfrac{5}{6}$ mile.

Reflect

2. **What If?** Would you model $1\frac{1}{4} \cdot \frac{2}{3}$ the same way as you modeled $\frac{2}{3} \cdot 1\frac{1}{4}$? Would the product be the same? Explain.

$\dfrac{2}{3},$

_____

_____

_____

_____

Multiplying Using a Number Line

You can use a number line to model the multiplication of fractions and mixed numbers, including negative numbers.

EXAMPLE

A **A carpenter is shaving down a door so that it will not stick. The tool she is using removes $\frac{1}{8}$–inch of wood with each pass. She runs the tool over the edge of the door 5 times. What is the change in the width of the door?**

Find $\left(-\frac{1}{8}\right)5$.

STEP 1 Use the Commutative Property to write $\left(-\frac{1}{8}\right)5$ as $5\left(-\frac{1}{8}\right)$.

> To show a negative number, move to the left on the number line.

STEP 2 Start at 0. Move $\frac{1}{8}$ unit to the left 5 times.

STEP 3 The result is $-\frac{5}{8}$.

The width of the door changes by $-\frac{5}{8}$ inch.

B **One batch of muffins requires $1\frac{2}{3}$ cups of flour. Tyrone needs to make 3 batches of muffins. How many cups of flour does he need?**

Find $\left(1\frac{2}{3}\right)3$.

STEP 1 Use the Commutative Property of Multiplication. $\left(1\frac{2}{3}\right)3 = 3\left(1\frac{2}{3}\right)$

STEP 2 Start at 0. Move $1\frac{2}{3}$ units to the right 3 times.

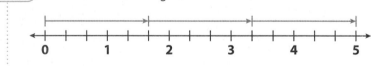

STEP 3 The result is 5.

Tyrone needs 5 cups of flour.

Reflect

3. **Error Analysis** Kristie says that the product of 2 and $1\frac{3}{4}$ is $1\frac{1}{2}$. Without doing the multiplication, how can you tell if Kristie's answer is correct?

_____

_____

_____

Use the grids or number line to find each product. Simplify products if needed.

1. $\frac{1}{2} \cdot \frac{1}{3} =$ _____

2. $\frac{1}{4} \cdot \frac{3}{4} =$ _____

3. $\frac{3}{4} \cdot \frac{2}{3} =$ _____

4. $\frac{1}{2} \cdot 1\frac{1}{3} =$ _____

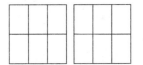

5. $\frac{3}{4} \cdot 1\frac{1}{2} =$ _____

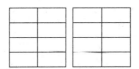

6. $\frac{1}{3} \cdot 1\frac{2}{3} =$ _____

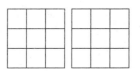

7. $3\left(-\frac{3}{4}\right) =$ _____

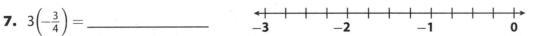

8. $2\left(1\frac{1}{3}\right) =$ _____

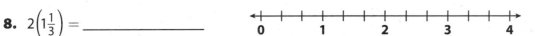

The table shows the amount of paint the drama club has for painting scenery. For 9–11, use the information in the table to write and simplify a multiplication expression. Use an area model or a number line if it is helpful.

9. Tobias used $\frac{3}{4}$ of the blue paint. How much blue paint did he use?

_____

Color	Amount (gal)
White	$1\frac{1}{2}$
Blue	2
Green	$1\frac{1}{4}$
Brown	$2\frac{3}{4}$

10. Janna mixed $\frac{1}{3}$ of the white paint with $\frac{1}{2}$ of the green paint. How many gallons of light green paint did she make?

_____

11. Three students each use $\frac{1}{2}$ gallon of brown paint. Then they buy 2 more gallons of brown paint. How much brown paint does the club have left?

_____

12. **Make a Conjecture** When you multiply two positive fractions that are each less than 1, is the product less than 1 or greater than 1? Explain.

_____

_____

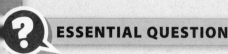

LESSON S.8 Determining a Proportional Relationship

How do you determine if a relationship is proportional when graphed?

EXPLORE ACTIVITY

Graphing Proportional Relationships

A **proportional relationship** is a relationship between two quantities in which the ratio of one quantity to the other is constant. If there is a proportional relationship between x and y, each x-value multiplied by a constant number results in the corresponding y-value.

A bird-cam is positioned to photograph a hawk's nest. While the camera is turned on, it records four images every hour.

A Explain why the relationship between number of images and number of hours is proportional. Describe the relationship in words.

_____

_____

_____

_____

B Complete the table.

Time (hours)	1	2	3		8
Images	4			20	32

C Write the data in the table as ordered pairs (time, images).

(1, 4), (2, _____), (3, _____), (_____, 20), (8, _____)

D Plot the ordered pairs on the coordinate grid.

E If the camera is used for 0 hours, how many images will be recorded? _____

What ordered pair represents this situation?

What is this location called? _____

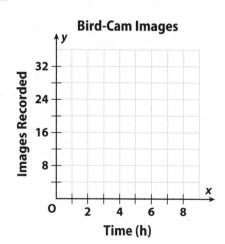

Bird-Cam Images

Reflect

1. **Analyze Relationships**   If the camera is used for 1 hour, how many images will be recorded? What ordered pair represents this situation? What is special about this ordered pair?

_____

2. If the camera is used for 12 hours, how many images will be recorded? _____

Identifying Proportional Relationships

You can use either a table or a graph to determine if a relationship is proportional. A relationship is a proportional relationship if its graph is a straight line through the origin.

EXAMPLE 1

The table shows the relationship between the cost of guitar lessons, in dollars, and the amount of lesson time in hours. Is the relationship a proportional relationship? If it is, identify the unit rate.

Time (h)	1	2	3	4	5
Cost ($)	35	70	105	140	175

Method 1 Represent the data in the table as ratios.

Write the ratio of cost to time for each pair of values. Then write each ratio in simplest form.

$\frac{cost(\$)}{time(h)}$: $\frac{35}{1} = \frac{35}{1}$ $\frac{70}{2} = \frac{35}{1}$ $\frac{105}{3} = \frac{35}{1}$ $\frac{140}{4} = \frac{35}{1}$ $\frac{175}{5} = \frac{35}{1}$

The ratios are all equivalent, so the relationship is proportional.

The constant ratio shows that the unit rate is $35 per hour.

Method 2 Represent the data in the table in a graph.

Write the data in the table as ordered pairs (time, cost).
(1, 35), (2, 70), (3, 105), (4, 140), (5, 175)
Graph the ordered pairs.

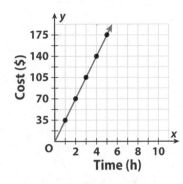

The graph is a line that goes through the origin, so the relationship is proportional.

The point (1, 35) on the graph shows that the unit rate is $35/hour.

Determining Whether a Relationship is Proportional

A relationship is proportional if its graph is a straight line that includes the origin. If its graph is not a straight line *or* does not go through the origin, the relationship is not proportional.

EXAMPLE 2

A Jared is 3 years older than his brother. Is the relationship between the brother's age and Jared's age a proportional relationship? Explain.

STEP 1 Create a table of values for Jared's age and his brother's age.

Brother's age (years)	0	1	2	3	6
Jared's age (years)	3	4	5	6	9

> Add 3 to the brother's age to find Jared's age.

STEP 2 Write the data in the table as ordered pairs (brother's age, Jared's age).

(0, 3), (1, 4), (2, 5), (3, 6), (6, 9)

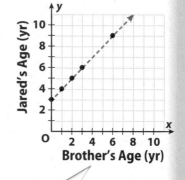

STEP 3 Graph the points and draw a line through them.

The graph is a straight line.

The graph does *not* go through the origin.

The relationship is *not* a proportional relationship.

> Notice that the ratio of Jared's age to his brother's age is *constant*.

B Mia kept a record of how many errands she ran for her grandmother and how many dollars her grandmother paid her. She wrote her data in a table:

Errands	0	2	3	5	7
Dollars	0	1	3	5	8

Is the relationship between the number of errands and dollars a proportional relationship? Explain.

STEP 1 Write the data in the table as ordered pairs.

(0, 0), (2, 1), (3, 3), (5, 5), (7, 8)

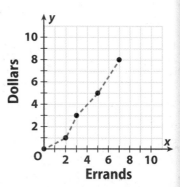

STEP 2 Graph the ordered pairs.

The graph includes the origin.

The points in the graph do *not* form a straight line.

The relationship is *not* a proportional relationship.

Represent the data in the table as ratios to determine whether the relationship is proportional or not. If it is, identify the unit rate.

1. The table shows the number of pencils bought for various amounts.

Pencils	2	5	9	20
Cost ($)	1.80	4.50	8.10	18

_____

_____

2. Kona makes $12.50 profit on each birdhouse that she makes and sells.

Number sold	2	3	6	8
Profit ($)	25			

_____

_____

Determine whether the relationship is a proportional relationship or not. Explain.

3.

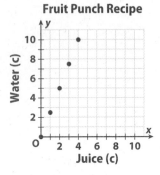

Fruit Punch Recipe

_____

_____

_____

4.

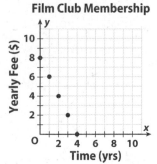

Film Club Membership

_____

_____

_____

Graph the points in each table. Explain whether the relationship is proportional.

5.

Books	2	4	7	10
Cost ($)	1	2	3.5	5

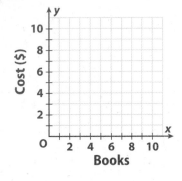

_____

_____

6.

Time (h)	1	3	6	9
Distance (mi)	50	190	250	375

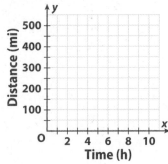

_____

_____

LESSON S.9 Comparing Percents

ESSENTIAL QUESTION

How can you compare two percents?

EXPLORE ACTIVITY 1

Comparing Percents Visually

Two classes are raising money to finance class trips. Each class sets a goal for how much money to raise, and they make a poster with a model to show how close they are to their goal. Which class has reached a greater percentage of their goal?

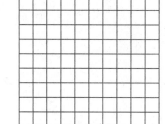

A Carol's class used the decimal grid to represent raising $60 out of their goal of $100. Shade the decimal grid to show how much money they have raised so far.

B What percent of their goal have they reached?

$$\frac{\text{Amount raised (\$)}}{\text{Goal (\$)}} = \frac{\boxed{}}{\boxed{}} = \underline{\hspace{1cm}} \%$$

Carol's class has raised _____ % of their goal.

C Shaun's class has a goal of raising $200. They used a bar model divided into 10 equal parts to represent how much money they have raised. Find out how much each bar represents and fill in the remaining labels.

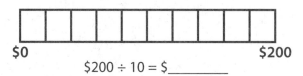

$0 $200

$200 ÷ 10 = $_____

D Shade the bar model above to show that Shaun's class has raised $80.

E What percent of their goal have they reached?

$$\frac{80}{200} = \frac{40}{100} = \underline{\hspace{1cm}} \%$$

Shaun's class has raised _____% of their goal.

F Describe two ways the classes can compare the percents shown by their models. Which class has reached a greater percent of their goal?

_____

_____

Reflect

1. **Analyze Relationships** How are the models made by the two classes similar?

_____

_____

Comparing Percents Symbolically

To compare two ratios, convert both of them to the same form. You can compare ratios written as percents, as decimals, or as fractions with the same denominator.

EXAMPLE 1

A Shandra and Maria set goals for how many books to read this summer. Who has reached a greater percent of her goal?

Shandra's Reading Goal: 10 books	Maria's Reading Goal: 15 books
‖‖ ‖	‖‖ ‖‖ ‖

STEP 1 Write the ratio of books read to the reading goal for each person.

Shandra: $\dfrac{6}{10}$ Maria: $\dfrac{12}{15}$

STEP 2 Write each ratio as a percent.

$$\overset{\times 10}{\dfrac{6}{10}} = \underset{\times 10}{\dfrac{60}{100}} = 60\%$$

$$\overset{\div 3}{\dfrac{12}{15}} = \overset{\times 20}{\dfrac{4}{5}} = \underset{\div 3 \quad \times 20}{\dfrac{80}{100}} = 80\%$$

> Writing the fraction in simplest form may make it easier to see how to write it with 100 in the denominator.

STEP 3 Compare the percents.

80% > 60%

Maria has reached a greater percent of her goal.

B Tarik's trail mix recipe uses 5 cups of dried fruit for every 6 cups of nuts. Arnav's recipe uses 7 cups of dried fruit for every 9 cups of nuts. Whose recipe has a greater proportion of dried fruit?

STEP 1 Write the ratio of fruit to nuts for each recipe.

Tarik: $\dfrac{5}{6}$ 　　　　　　　　Arnav: $\dfrac{7}{9}$

STEP 2 Write the two ratios as fractions with the same denominator.

$\times 3$

$$\dfrac{5}{6} = \dfrac{15}{18}$$

$\times 3$

$\times 2$

$$\dfrac{7}{9} = \dfrac{14}{18}$$

$\times 2$

> The least common multiple of 6 and 9 is 18. Use 18 as the denominator.

STEP 3 Compare the fractions.

$$\dfrac{15}{18} > \dfrac{14}{18}$$

Tarik's trail mix has a greater proportion of dried fruit.

Comparing Percents

To compare proportions represented with two different models, write both of them as percents, then compare.

EXAMPLE 2

Identify the percent shown in each of the two models. Then compare the percents. Assume that each model is divided into equal parts.

STEP 1 Write the fraction that each model represents.

The bar model shows 7 out of 9 parts shaded, or $\dfrac{7}{9}$.

The circle model shows 3 out of 4 parts shaded, or $\dfrac{3}{4}$.

STEP 2 Write each fraction as a percent.

$$\dfrac{7}{9} = 77\dfrac{7}{9}\%$$ 　　　　　$$\dfrac{3}{4} = 0.75 = 75\%$$

> Use benchmark percents or use long division to convert fractions to percents.

STEP 3 Compare the percents.

$$77\dfrac{7}{9}\% > 75\%$$

The bar model shows the greater percent.

Identify the percent shown by each of the two models. Then compare using the >, <, or = symbols. Assume that each model is divided into equal parts.

1. 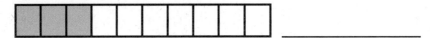 _____

2. 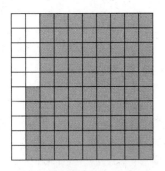  _____

3.  _____

4. 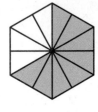 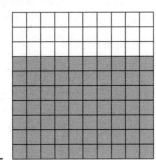 _____

5. 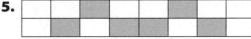 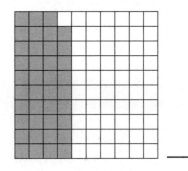 _____

6. Kira answered 45 questions correctly on a 50-question test, and she answered 13 questions correctly on a 20-question quiz. Write both scores as percents, then compare the percents. Did she score a higher percentage on the test or the quiz?

_____

7. In Ms. Markman's class, 18 out of 27 students ate the cafeteria lunch. In Mr. Lee's class, 24 out of 36 students ate the cafeteria lunch. Compare the fraction of students in each class who ate the cafeteria lunch.

_____

8. A chemist has two solutions. Flask A contains 25 ml of isopropanol in 500 ml of solution. Flask B contains 16 ml of isopropanol in 200 ml of solution. What is the percent of isopropanol in each flask? Which is greater?

_____

Perfect Squares

? ESSENTIAL QUESTION

How can you recognize a perfect square?

EXPLORE ACTIVITY 1

Exploring Patterns in Squares

The formula for the area of a square is $A = s \times s$, or $A = s^2$, where s represents the side length. The exponent 2 tells the number of times s is used as a factor.

Use the area formula to find the areas of squares of various sizes.

A Find the area of the square shown.

$A = s \times s$

$= \boxed{} \times \boxed{}$ *Substitute the side length for s.*

$= \boxed{}^{\boxed{}}$ *Write using an exponent.*

$= \boxed{}$ square units   *Simplify.*

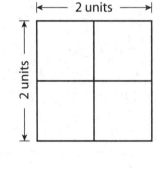

B Complete the first row of the table below.

Square	Area Expressed Using an Exponent (square units)	Area (square units)
2 × 2	2²	
3 × 3		
4 × 4		

C Use graph paper to sketch a 3 × 3 square and a 4 × 4 square. Find the area of each square and express it using an exponent. Record your answers in the table.

D Draw four squares of different sizes on graph paper. Find their areas. Record the information about your squares in the next four rows of the table.

Reflect

1. Describe any pattern you see in the table.

_____

_____

_____

2. **What if?** Suppose you want to make a grid with whole-number side lengths that has an area of 15 square units. Could the grid be a square? Explain.

_____

_____

_____

Identifying Perfect Squares

When a number is *squared*, it is multiplied by itself. A **perfect square** is the product of a whole number multiplied by itself.

EXAMPLE 1

Express each number as a product of two factors in as many ways as possible. Then determine whether the number is a perfect square.

A **36**

Identify the factor pairs for 36:

1×36 $\quad$ 2×18 $\quad$ 3×12 $\quad$ 4×9 $\quad$ (6×6)

36×1 $\quad$ 18×2 $\quad$ 12×3 $\quad$ 9×4

The factor pair 6×6 is a whole number multiplied by itself.

36 is a *perfect square*.

B **12**

Identify the factor pairs for 12:

1×12 $\quad$ 2×6 $\quad$ 3×4 $\quad$ 4×3 $\quad$ 6×2 $\quad$ 12×1

No factor pair of 12 is a whole number multiplied by itself.

12 is *not* a perfect square.

My Notes

Applying Perfect Squares to Solve a Problem

Identifying perfect squares can help you solve problems.

EXAMPLE 2

A **Alexandra has 225 square tiles of the same size. Could she use all the tiles to make a square design?**

Identify factor pairs for 225:

1×225 3×75 5×45 9×25 15×15

Since $15 \times 15 = 225$, the tiles could be arranged in 15 rows of 15 tiles each, making a square design.

B **A builder has 264 patio tiles that measure 1 square foot each. Could a square patio be made using all the tiles? If so, what is the length of each side?**

Use familiar numbers to find a range of possible side lengths.

$10 \times 10 = 100$ and $20 \times 20 = 400$,

so the side length must be between 10 and 20.

Find the squares of integers greater than 10.

$11 \times 11 = 121$ $12 \times 12 = 144$ $13 \times 13 = 169$

$14 \times 14 = 196$ $15 \times 15 = 225$ $16 \times 16 = 256$

$17 \times 17 = 289$

> Knowing multiplication facts will help you recognize perfect squares.

264 is greater than 16×16 and less than 17×17, so it is not a perfect square.

The patio could not be a square.

Reflect

3. **Communicate Mathematical Ideas** In Part B, how could you have further narrowed down the range of possible side lengths to find the squares?

_____

_____

_____

Use the grid to determine whether the given area could be the area of a square with a whole-number side length. If it is possible, express the area using an exponent.

1. 49 square units

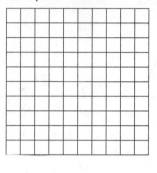

_____

2. 24 square units

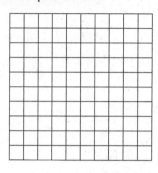

_____

Identify whether each number is a perfect square. If it is, express the area of the square using an exponent.

3. 81

_____

4. 48

_____

5. 72

_____

6. 196

_____

7. 56

_____

8. 14,400

_____

9. Mr. Carrey wants to arrange the desks in his classroom so that there are the same number of rows as columns of desks. Is this arrangement possible with 30 desks? If not, how many desks does he need to remove to make it possible? Explain.

_____

_____

_____

10. An artist is using 1-foot-square tiles to design a square mosaic for a wall that is 20 feet high and 24 feet long. The mosaic must have an area of at least 220 square feet. How many different sizes of mosaic are possible? Explain.

_____

_____

_____

_____

LESSON
S.11 Powers of 10

? ESSENTIAL QUESTION

How can you use an exponent to show powers of 10?

EXPLORE ACTIVITY

Identifying Patterns in Powers of 10

Expressions with repeated factors, such as $10 \times 10 \times 10$, can be written by using a base with an exponent. A **power of 10** is a number formed by repeated multiplication by 10. For example, $10 \times 10 \times 10$ is 10^3. You can read 10^3 as 10 raised to the third power, or the third power of 10.

A Complete the table to show powers of 10.

Power of 10	Product	Exponential Form
1×10	10	10^1
$1 \times 10 \times 10$		
$1 \times 10 \times 10 \times 10$		
$1 \times 10 \times 10 \times 10 \times 10$		

B Compare the middle column and the last column. What relationship do you see between the exponent and the zeros in the product?

_____

_____

Reflect

1. **Communicate Mathematical Ideas** In a power, the exponent tells how many times the base is multiplied by itself. This also applies to powers of 10. Complete the statement.

   The exponent on 10 tells you how many times _____ is used as a factor and how many _____ are in the product.

© Houghton Mifflin Harcourt Publishing Company

Multiplying a Whole Number by a Power of 10

To multiply a whole number by a power of 10, use the patterns in the table.

EXAMPLE

Krill, a small shrimp-like animal found in the ocean, is a favorite food of the blue whale. An adult blue whale may eat as much as 8×10^3 pounds of krill in a day. How much krill is that, written as a whole number?

Multiply 8 by powers of ten using a pattern.

$8 \times 10^0 = 8 \times 1 = 8$

$8 \times 10^1 = 8 \times 10 = 80$

$8 \times 10^2 = 8 \times 10 \times 10 = 800$

$8 \times 10^3 = 8 \times 10 \times 10 \times 10 = 8,000$

So, an adult blue whale may eat as much as 8,000 pounds of krill in a day.

Practice

Write the exponential form for each product.

1. $1 \times 10 \times 10 \times 10 \times 10 \times 10$ _____

2. $4 \times 10 \times 10$ _____

3. $7 \times 10 \times 10 \times 10 \times 10 \times 10$ _____

4. 8 _____

5. 3×10 _____

6. $2 \times 10 \times 10 \times 10 \times 10$ _____

7. $5 \times 10 \times 10 \times 10 \times 10 \times 10 \times 10 \times 10$ _____

Find the value, written as a whole number, for each expression.

8. 10^6 _____

9. 7×10^0 _____

10. 13×10^1 _____

11. 4×10^3 _____

12. 8×10^5 _____

13. 10^7 _____

14. 10^8 _____

15. 43×10^4 _____

16. An adult blue whale can eat up to 4×10^7 individual krill in a day. How many krill is that, written as a whole number? _____

17. In 2003, Earth and Mars were the closest they have been in 50,000 years, when they were about 33,900,000 miles apart. Write this distance as a whole number multiplied by a power of ten.

_____

Identifying the Solution Set of an Inequality

? ESSENTIAL QUESTION How do you determine if a numerical value is part of the solution set of a given inequality?

EXPLORE ACTIVITY 1

Solving Inequalities Using Addition

Just as the two sides of an equation remain equal when you add or subtract the same number on both sides, the two sides of an inequality keep the same "less than" or "greater than" relationship when you add or subtract the same number on both sides. You can use this property to find the solutions of an inequality.

After Orlando spent $7 for lunch, he had less than $5 left in his pockets. How much did he have in his pockets before he paid for his lunch?

A Choose a variable and describe what it means.

Let x represent the amount of money, in dollars, that

_____

B Write an inequality to represent the situation.

$x - \boxed{} < \boxed{}$

C Add the same number to both sides of the inequality.

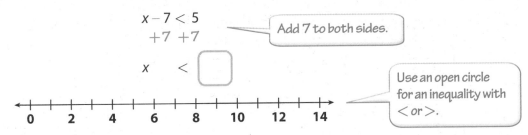

$$x - 7 < 5$$
$$+7 \quad +7$$

Add 7 to both sides.

$$x \quad < \boxed{}$$

Use an open circle for an inequality with $<$ or $>$.

0 2 4 6 8 10 12 14

D Graph the solutions on a number line.

E Interpret the result.

Orlando had _____ in his pockets before he paid for lunch.

Reflect

1. **What if?** Suppose Orlando had less than $8 in his pockets after spending $7 for lunch. How much did he have in his pockets before he paid for lunch?

_____

Solving Inequalities Using Subtraction

The **solution set** of an equation or inequality is the set of numbers that makes the equation or inequality true.

EXAMPLE 1

A **Solve $13 \leq y + 4$. Then graph the solution set.**

$13 \leq y + 4$ Write the inequality.

$\underline{-4 \qquad -4}$ Subtract 4 from both sides.

$9 \leq y$
or
$y \geq 9$

> If you reverse the direction of an inequality, remember to reverse the inequality sign.

The solution set is the set of all numbers greater than or equal to 9.

Graph the solution set on a number line. Since 9 must be included in the solution set, use a closed circle.

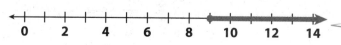

> Use a closed circle for an inequality with $\leq$ or $\geq$.

B **Between 5 a.m and 8 a.m, the temperature rose by 7 ºF. At 8 a.m, the temperature was less than −4 ºF. What was the temperature at 5 a.m?**

Let t be the temperature at 5 a.m, in ºF.

$t + 7 <\ -4$ Write an inequality representing the situation.

$\underline{-7 \qquad -7}$ Subtract 7 from both sides.

$t \qquad <\ -11$

The solution set is the set of all numbers less than −11. Since −11 is not included in the solution set, use an open circle.

Graph the solution set on a number line.

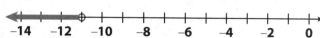

Interpret the solution.

The temperature at 5 a.m was less than −11 ºF.

Reflect

2. **Communicate Mathematical Ideas** Explain why the inequality $9 \leq y$ is equivalent to $y \geq 9$.

_____

_____

_____

Determining Whether a Number is a Solution to an Inequality

To determine whether a given number is a solution to an inequality, substitute the number for the variable in the inequality. If the number makes the inequality true, then it is a solution. If the number makes the inequality false, then it is not a solution.

EXAMPLE 2

Determine if each value is a solution of the inequality.

A Is 11 a solution to $b - 3 \leq 8$?

$b - 3 \leq 8$	Write the inequality.
$11 - 3 \overset{?}{\leq} 8$	Substitute 11 for b.
$8 \overset{?}{\leq} 8$	Subtract.

Is 8 less than or equal to 8?

Since $8 \leq 8$ is true, 11 is a solution of $b - 3 \leq 8$.

B Is −6 a solution to $5 + c < -3$?

$5 + c < -3$	Write the inequality.
$5 + (-6) \overset{?}{<} -3$	Substitute −6 for c.
$-1 \overset{?}{<} -3$	Add.

Is −1 less than −3?

Since $-1 < -3$ is false, −6 is not a solution of $5 + c < -3$.

CHECK: You can also see that this answer makes sense by solving $5 + c < -3$ and graphing the solution set.

$$5 + c < -3$$
$$\underline{-5 \qquad -5}$$
$$c < -8$$

The solution is the set of all numbers less than −8.

Graph the solution set and graph the number −6.

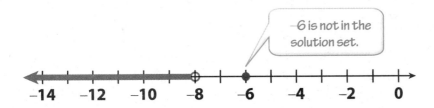

−6 is not in the solution set.

You can see that −6 is not in the solution set of $5 + c < -3$.

Solve. Then graph the solution set.

1. $m - 6 \leq 3$ _____

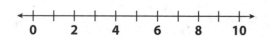

2. $n + 3 > -4$ _____

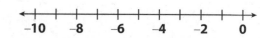

3. $p - 4 < -5$ _____

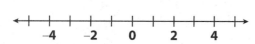

4. $8 \leq q + 2$ _____

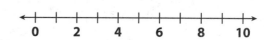

5. $r + 5 \leq 2$ _____

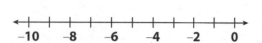

6. $4 < s - 7$ _____

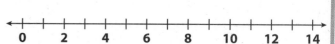

Determine whether the given value is a solution of the inequality $d + 3 > -2$.

7. −2

_____

8. −5

_____

9. −1

_____

Determine whether the given value is a solution of the inequality $k - 4 \leq -3$.

10. −2

_____

11. 1

_____

12. 3

_____

Choose a variable and write an inequality to represent the situation. Solve the inequality and interpret the result.

13. Fatima withdrew $15 from her savings account. Afterward, she had at most $24 in the account. How much did she have in the account before she made the withdrawal?

_____

_____

_____

14. Between 4 a.m and 9 a.m, the temperature increased 10 °F. At 9 a.m, the temperature was greater than −6 °F. What was the temperature at 4 a.m?

_____

_____

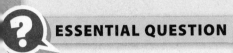

LESSON S.13 Graphing on the Coordinate Plane

? **ESSENTIAL QUESTION**

How do you locate and name points in the coordinate plane?

EXPLORE ACTIVITY

Naming Points in the Coordinate Plane

A coordinate plane is formed by two number lines that intersect at right angles. The point of intersection is 0 on each number line.

- The two number lines are called the **axes**.

- The horizontal axis is called the **x-axis**.

- The vertical axis is called the **y-axis**.

- The point where the axes intersect is called the **origin**.

- The two axes divide the coordinate plane into four **quadrants**.

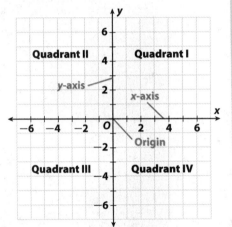

An **ordered pair** is a pair of numbers that gives the location of a point on a coordinate plane. The first number tells how far to the right (positive) or left (negative) the point is located from the origin. The second number tells how far up (positive) or down (negative) the point is located from the origin.

The numbers in an ordered pair are called **coordinates**. The first number is the **x-coordinate**, and the second number is the **y-coordinate**.

A Identify the coordinates of each point. Name the quadrant where each point is located.

Point A is 1 unit _____ of the origin and 5 units _____.

It has x-coordinate _____ and y-coordinate _____,

written _____. It is located in Quadrant _____.

Point B is 2 units _____ of the origin and 3 units _____.

It has x-coordinate _____ and y-coordinate _____,

written _____. It is located in Quadrant _____.

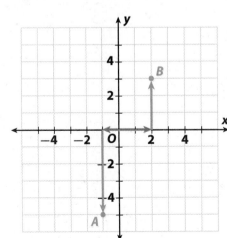

B Identify the coordinates of each point. Identify where each point is located.

Point *C* is 3 units _____ of the origin. It has

x-coordinate ____ and *y*-coordinate ____, written _____.

It is located in _____ of the quadrants.

It is on the ____-axis.

Point *D* is 5 units _____ from the origin.

It has *x*-coordinate ____ and *y*-coordinate _____ , written _____ .

It is located in _____ of the quadrants. It is on the _____-axis.

Reflect

1. **Communicate Mathematical Ideas** Explain why (−3, 5) represents a different location than (3, 5).

_____

_____

Graphing Points in the Coordinate Plane

Points that are located on the axes are not located in any quadrant. Points on the *x*-axis have a *y*-coordinate of 0, and points on the *y*-axis have an *x*-coordinate of 0.

EXAMPLE 1

Graph and label each point on the coordinate plane.

A(−5, 2), *B*(3, 5), *C*(0,−3)

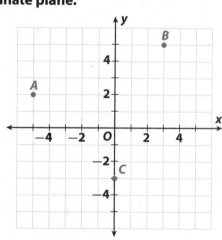

Point *A* is 5 units *left* and 2 units *up* from the origin.

Point *B* is 3 units *right* and 5 units *up* from the origin.

Point *C* is 3 units *down* from the origin, so it is graphed on the *y*-axis.

Reflect

2. **Communicate Mathematical Ideas** Which of these points is not located in any quadrant: $P(-4, 2)$, $Q(3, 2)$, $R(-4, -5)$, $S(4, -5)$, or $T(-2, 0)$? Explain how you know.

_____

Reading Scales on Axes

The scale of an axis is the number of units that each grid line represents. So far, the graphs in this lesson have had a scale of 1 unit, but graphs frequently use other scales.

EXAMPLE 2

The graph shows the location of a city. It also shows the location of Gary's and Jen's houses. The scale on each axis represents miles.

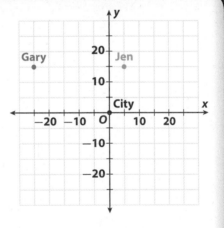

A Use the scale to describe Gary's location relative to the city.

Each grid square is 5 miles on a side.

Gary's house is at $(-25, 15)$, which is 25 miles west and 15 miles north of the city.

B Describe the location of Jen's house relative to Gary's house.

Jen's house is located 6 grid squares to the right of Gary's house. Since each grid square is 5 miles on a side, her house is $6 \times 5 = 30$ miles east of Gary's.

Reflect

3. **What If?** Suppose Vinh lives near the same city as Gary and Jen. Vinh's apartment is 15 miles south and 15 miles west of the city. His new job is 25 miles to the east of his apartment. Give the coordinates for Vinh's apartment and his job.

_____

4. **Analyze Relationships** What do you know about the coordinates of two points that both lie on the same vertical line through the coordinate plane?

_____

_____

Identify the coordinates of each point. Name the quadrant where each point is located.

1. Point A is 5 units _____ of the origin and

   1 unit _____ from the origin.

   Its coordinates are _____. It is in quadrant _____.

2. Point B is _____ units right of the origin

   and _____ units down from the origin.

   Its coordinates are _____. It is in quadrant _____.

Graph and label each point on the coordinate plane above.

3. Point C at (−2, 3)

4. Point D at (5, 0)

For 5—7, use the coordinate plane shown.

5. Describe the scale of the graph.

   _____

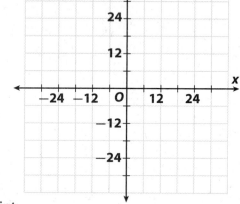

6. Graph and label point A at (−6, 24).

7. Graph and label point B at (30, −18).

8. **Vocabulary** Describe how an ordered pair represents a point
   on a coordinate plane. Include the terms *x-coordinate*, *y-coordinate*, and *origin* in your answer.

   _____

   _____

   _____

9. Zach graphs some ordered pairs in the coordinate plane. The *x*-values of the ordered pairs
   represent the time of day, and the *y*-values represent the temperature at that time. In what
   quadrants could Zach graph points? Explain your thinking.

   _____

   _____

   _____

   _____

LESSON S.14 Regular Polygons

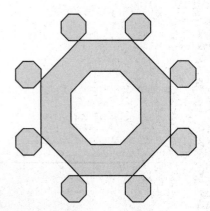

? ESSENTIAL QUESTION

How can you identify and classify polygons?

EXPLORE ACTIVITY 1

Identifying Polygons

A **polygon** is a closed figure formed by three or more line segments that meet at points called vertices. It is named by the number of sides and angles it has.

The Castel del Monte in Apulia, Italy, was built more than 750 years ago. The fortress has one central building with eight surrounding towers. Which polygon do you see repeated in the structure? How many sides, angles, and vertices does this polygon have?

A Complete the tables below.

Polygon	Triangle	Quadrilateral	Pentagon	Hexagon
Sides	3	4	5	
Angles				
Vertices				

Polygon	Heptagon	Octagon	Nonagon	Decagon
Sides	7	8		
Angles				
Vertices				

B Identify the repeated polygon in the fortress.

The _____ is the repeated polygon in the Castel del Monte because it has _____ sides, _____ angles, and _____ vertices.

Reflect

1. **Look for a Pattern** What pattern do you see among the number of sides, angles, and vertices a polygon has?

_____

_____

Classifying Polygons

When line segments have the same length or when angles have the same measure, they are **congruent**. Two polygons are congruent when they have the same size and the same shape. In a **regular polygon**, all sides are congruent and all angles are congruent.

| **regular polygon** All sides are congruent. All angles are congruent. | 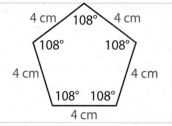 | **irregular polygon** Not all sides are congruent. Not all angles are congruent. | 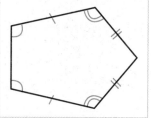 |

A Label the Venn Diagram to classify the polygons in each group.

Congruent · · · · · · Regular · · · · · · Congruent

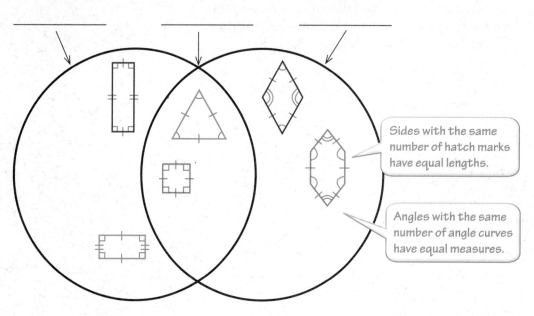

Sides with the same number of hatch marks have equal lengths.

Angles with the same number of angle curves have equal measures.

B Draw another polygon for each section of the diagram.

_____

Reflect

2. Analyze Relationships How does the group of polygons in the center section of the Venn diagram relate to the groups in the left and right sections of the diagram?

_____
_____
_____

Naming Polygons

When you name a polygon, identify the type of polygon and whether it is a regular polygon or an irregular polygon.

EXAMPLE

Name each polygon and identify it as a regular or an irregular polygon.

A
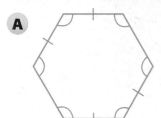
The figure has 6 sides and 6 angles.
All the sides are congruent.
All the angles are congruent.
The figure is a regular hexagon.

B
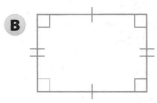
The figure has 4 sides and 4 angles.
Not all of the sides are congruent.
All the angles are congruent.
The figure is an irregular quadrilateral.

> A rectangle is an irregular polygon because all sides are not congruent.

C
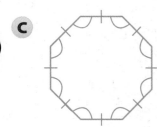
The figure has 8 sides and 8 angles.
All the sides are congruent.
All the angles are congruent.
The figure is a regular octagon.

Reflect

3. What is the name of a regular quadrilateral? Explain.

_____

_____

_____

4. **Justify Reasoning** In Part B, all the angles are congruent but not all the sides are congruent. Can a polygon have all congruent sides but not all congruent angles? Explain.

_____

_____

Name each polygon and identify it as a regular or an irregular polygon.

1.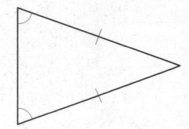

_____

2.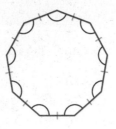

_____

3.

_____

4.

_____

5.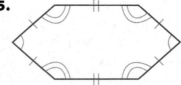

_____

6.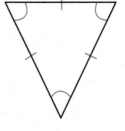

_____

7. A designer is using the shapes shown below in a stained glass window. Compare the polygons. Explain how they are alike and how they are different.

_____

_____

_____

_____

_____

_____

8. Amal is making a pattern using the polygons shown. Name the polygons and identify them as regular or irregular. Do they have the same shape? If so, why?

_____

_____

_____

LESSON
S.15 Lines of Symmetry

? ESSENTIAL QUESTION

How can you use lines of symmetry to divide regular polygons?

EXPLORE ACTIVITY 1

Exploring Line Symmetry

A shape has **line symmetry** if it can be folded about a line so that its two parts line up and match exactly.

A fold line, or a **line of symmetry**, divides a shape into two parts that are the same size and shape.

Is each line a line of symmetry? If not, explain why.

A

_____

_____

B

_____

_____

C

_____

_____

D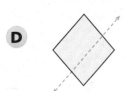

_____

_____

Reflect

1. **Critical Thinking** Does the triangle from Part C have any line symmetry? Explain.

_____

_____

Lines of Symmetry

A polygon may have more than one line of symmetry.

Find all the lines of symmetry for each figure.

A Isosceles Triangle

B Equilateral Triangle

STEP 1 Fold the triangle to test for line symmetry.	**STEP 1** Fold the triangle to test for line symmetry.

The fold line is a line of symmetry

The fold line is a line of symmetry.

STEP 2 Mark the line of symmetry	**STEP 2** Mark the line of symmetry.

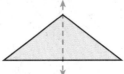

STEP 3 Rotate the triangle. Can you draw another line of symmetry?	**STEP 3** Rotate the triangle. Can you draw another line of symmetry?

No; if the triangle is folded along any other side, the two parts do not match exactly.

Repeat to find all lines of symmetry.

STEP 4 Identify the total number of lines of symmetry.	**STEP 4** Identify the total number of lines of symmetry.

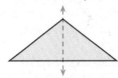

An isosceles triangle has one line of symmetry.

An equilateral triangle has three lines of symmetry.

Drawing Lines of Symmetry

A polygon may have zero, one, or more than one line of symmetry.

A Draw all the lines of symmetry for each figure in the table.

Polygon	Number of Sides	Number of Lines of Symmetry
equilateral triangle	3	3
square		
rhombus		
parallelogram		
regular hexagon		

B Complete the table. Identify the number of sides and the number of lines of symmetry each figure has.

Reflect

2. **Look for a Pattern** Which of the polygons in the table are regular polygons? What do you notice about the number of lines of symmetry in regular polygons? How can you test your observation?

_____

_____

_____

Practice

Is the dashed line a line of symmetry?

1.

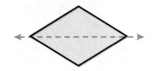

_____

2.

_____

3.

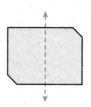

_____

Does the shape have line symmetry? If so, draw all lines of symmetry. Write the number of lines of symmetry for each shape.

4.

_____

5.

_____

6.

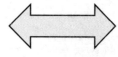

_____

7.

_____

8.

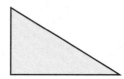

_____

9.

_____

10. How many lines of symmetry does the stop sign have, both with and without considering the word written on it? How many lines of symmetry does each letter on the stop sign have? Explain, using a picture if needed.

_____

_____

_____

_____

_____

11. A radiation warning sign is shown at the right. How many lines of symmetry does the sign have, considering the figure on the interior? Explain.

_____

_____

_____

? **ESSENTIAL QUESTION**

How do you use properties of polygons to determine the congruence of segments and angles in polygons?

EXPLORE ACTIVITY 1

Properties of Quadrilaterals

A quadrilateral is a polygon with four sides and four angles.

> Matching hash marks indicate sides that have the same length. In this figure, opposite sides have equal length.

When describing quadrilaterals, *opposite sides* are a pair of sides that do not connect to each other. In the figure shown, sides $\overline{AB}$ and $\overline{CD}$ are opposite sides, and sides $\overline{AD}$ and $\overline{BC}$ are opposite sides.

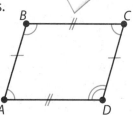

Similarly, angles *A* and *C* are *opposite angles*, and angles *B* and *D* are opposite angles.

The table describes properties of the sides and angles of common quadrilaterals.

On each figure, mark any right angles, add angle marks to show congruent angles, and add hash marks to show congruent sides.

Quadrilateral		Sides	Angles
Square		• All 4 sides have equal length. • Opposite sides are parallel.	4 right angles
Rhombus		• All 4 sides have equal length. • Opposite sides are parallel.	Opposite angles are congruent.
Rectangle		• Opposite sides have equal length. • Opposite sides are parallel.	4 right angles
Parallelogram		• Opposite sides have equal length. • Opposite sides are parallel.	Opposite angles are congruent.
Trapezoid		• Exactly 1 pair of opposite sides is parallel.	

EXPLORE ACTIVITY 1 *(cont'd)*

Reflect

1. **Critical Thinking** Which quadrilateral shown in the table has no congruent sides or angles? Is it possible to draw an example of that type of quadrilateral that *does* have a pair of congruent sides? If so, sketch an example.

____

EXPLORE ACTIVITY 2

Properties of Triangles

Triangles can be named based on the properties of their sides or their angles.

Sketch an example of each type of triangle named below. Mark congruent sides, congruent angles, and right angles.

Triangle	Properties
Equilateral Triangle	• All 3 sides have the same length. All 3 angles are congruent.
Isosceles Triangle	• 2 sides have the same length. 2 angles are congruent.
Scalene Triangle	• All sides have different lengths. All angles have different measures.
Right Triangle	• One angle is a right angle.

Reflect

2. **Draw Conclusions** Is an equilateral triangle a regular polygon? Explain.

____

____

Identifying Congruent Segments and Angles

You can use the properties of polygons to draw conclusions about congruent segments and angles. The symbol ≅ means "is congruent to" and can be used to indicate that segments, angles, or polygons are congruent.

EXAMPLE

A **Triangle *ABC* is an equilateral triangle. Quadrilateral *ACDE* is a square.**

Which segments are congruent to $\overline{AB}$?

By the definition of an equilateral triangle, segments $\overline{AB}$, $\overline{BC}$, and $\overline{AC}$ are congruent.

$$\overline{AB} \cong \overline{BC} \cong \overline{AC}$$

> We can write a congruency statement to show segments that are equal.

By the definition of a square, $\overline{AC}$, $\overline{CD}$, $\overline{ED}$, and $\overline{AE}$ are congruent.

$$\overline{AC} \cong \overline{CD} \cong \overline{ED} \cong \overline{AE}$$

Since $\overline{AC}$ is congruent to $\overline{AB}$, all the segments in the figure are congruent to $\overline{AB}$.

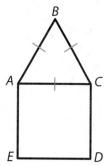

B **Quadrilateral *FGHJ* is a rectangle. Find angle measures *a*, *b*, *c*. Then identify angles congruent to ∠*FJG*.**

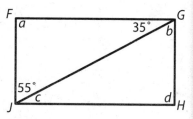

All four angles in a rectangle are right angles, so *a* and *d* are each 90°.

Angles *JGH* and *FGJ* together make a right angle.

$b + 35° = 90°$ Right angle

$b = 55°$ Subtract 35 from both sides.

Angles *GJH* and *FJG* together make a right angle.

$c + 55° = 90°$ Right angle

$c = 35°$ Subtract 55 from both sides.

The angle measures are $a = 90°$, $b = 55°$, $c = 35°$, and $d = 90°$.
∠*FJG* and ∠*JGH* both have angle measures of 55°, so ∠*FJG* ∠*JGH*.

Practice

Write the name of each figure. If more than one name applies, list both.

1.

2.

3.

_____ _____ _____

Identify the congruent sides or angles in each figure by writing a congruency statement.

4. Triangle *PQS* and triangle *QRS* are congruent right triangles. Which segments are congruent to $\overline{PS}$?

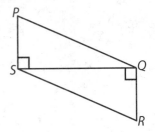

_____

5. *TUWX* is a parallelogram. Triangle *UVW* is isosceles. Which angles are congruent to ∠*UVW*?

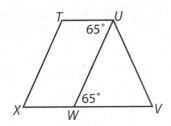

_____

6. Quadrilaterals *EFGK* and *GHJK* are rectangles. Which segments are congruent to $\overline{JH}$?

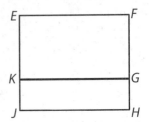

_____

7. The dashed line is a line of symmetry, and it divides the figure into two parallelograms. Which angles are congruent to ∠*LMP*?

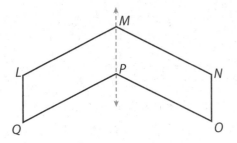

_____

8. Triangles *ABC* and *ACD* are equilateral triangles. What are the measures of angles *B* and *D*? What type of quadrilateral is *ABCD*? Explain.

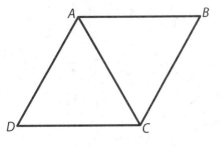

_____

_____

_____

_____

_____

9. Mr. Walker's garden has the shape of a rectangle and a square put together, as shown. What is the length of the fence?

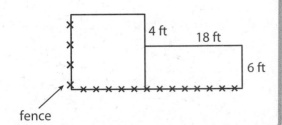

fence

_____

? **ESSENTIAL QUESTION**

How do you determine whether two polygons are congruent?

EXPLORE ACTIVITY

Identifying Congruence of Quadrilaterals

Corresponding parts of polygons are sides or angles that are in the same relative position in each polygon. In congruent polygons, *corresponding sides* are the same length and *corresponding angles* have the same angle measure. For two polygons to be congruent, they must have the same number of sides and their corresponding parts must be congruent.

Examine the quadrilaterals below. Recall that congruent polygons have the same size and same shape.

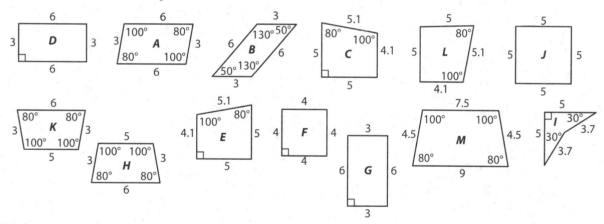

A Shade in polygons that are congruent.

B *C* is congruent to _____ and _____, *D* is congruent to _____, and _____ is congruent to _____.

C Which pairs of polygons have the same shape but have unequal corresponding side lengths ? _____

In polygons with the same shape, the measures of corresponding angles are | equal | not equal |.

Polygons whose corresponding angles have equal measures but whose corresponding side lengths are not equal are | congruent | noncongruent .|

D Which polygons do not have the same shape as any other polygon? How do you know?

_____

_____

Reflect

1. **Justify Reasoning** Why is it necessary to check that both the corresponding sides and the corresponding angles are congruent?

_____

_____

_____

Determining Whether Two Figures are Congruent

Compare corresponding parts to decide whether two figures are congruent.

EXAMPLE

Determine whether the two figures are congruent. If they are, write a correct congruency statement.

A

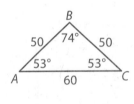 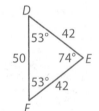

STEP 1 Compare corresponding angle measures.

$m\angle A = m\angle D = 53°$ $m\angle B = m\angle E = 74°$ $m\angle C = m\angle F = 53°$

All corresponding angles have the same measure, so the corresponding angles are congruent.

$\angle A \cong \angle D$ $\angle B \cong \angle E$ $\angle C \cong \angle F$

STEP 2 Identify and compare corresponding sides.

> If any corresponding parts are not congruent, the figures are not congruent.

$AB = 50$ but $DE = 42$; $AB \neq DE$, and so AB is not congruent to DE. Similarly, BC and EF have different measures, and also $AC \neq DF$, so those pairs of corresponding sides are not congruent.

There is at least one pair of corresponding sides that are not congruent; therefore, triangles ABC and DEF are noncongruent.

B

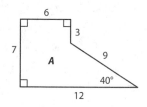

(figure at top showing two congruent quadrilaterals ABCD and EFGH with "congruent sides", "congruent angles" labels)

STEP 1 Identify and compare corresponding sides.

> You can compare either sides or angles first.

The hatch marks identifying equal side lengths indicate that corresponding sides are congruent.

STEP 2 Identify and compare corresponding angles.

The angle curves identifying equal angle measures indicate that corresponding angles are congruent.

The two figures are congruent. Since *A* corresponds with *E*, *B* with *F*, *C* with *G*, and *D* with *H*, write *ABCD* ≅ *EFGH*.

Practice

1. Shade in the figures that are congruent.

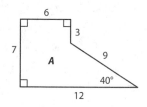
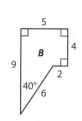
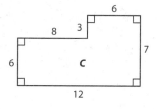
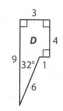
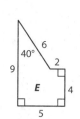

Determine whether the figures are congruent or noncongruent. If they are, write a correct congruency statement.

2.

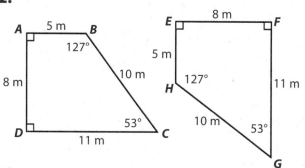

3.

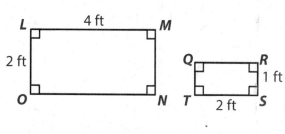

4.

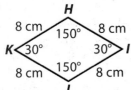 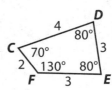

5.

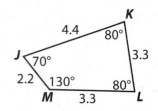

_____   _____

6.

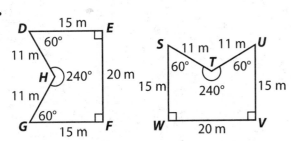 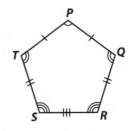

7.

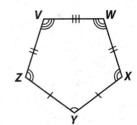

_____   _____

8. Draw Conclusions A climbing dome is made of regular hexagonal shapes. Each side of the hexagon is the same length. Each angle inside the hexagon has the same measure. Bars from each corner of the hexagon meet at the center of the hexagon. What, if anything, can you conclude about the triangles formed inside the hexagon? Explain.

_____

_____

9. Caleb had the tiles shown below. Are any of the tiles congruent? How do you know?

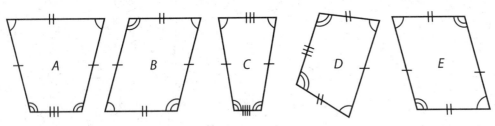

_____

_____

_____

Circumference and Perimeter

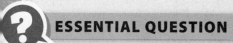

ESSENTIAL QUESTION

How do you find the circumference of a circle?

EXPLORE ACTIVITY 1

Exploring Circumference

A circle is a set of points in a plane that are a fixed distance from a point called the center.

The **circumference** of a circle is the distance around the circle.

The **diameter** of a circle is the length of a line segment that passes through the center of the circle with both endpoints on the circle.

The **radius** of a circle is the distance from the center of the circle to any point on the circle. The radius is half the diameter of the circle.

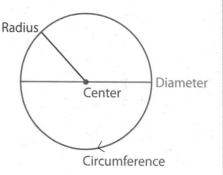

Follow the steps below to explore the relationship between the circumference, diameter, and radius of a circle.

A Gather four circular objects. Use a metric measuring tape to find the circumference C and the diameter d of each object to the nearest tenth of a centimeter. Record each measure in the table.

Object	Circumference C	Diameter d	$\dfrac{C}{d}$
soup can	27 cm	8.5 cm	$\dfrac{27}{8.5} \approx 3.18$

B Divide the circumference C of each object by its diameter d. Round the quotient to the nearest hundredth. Record the answer in the $\dfrac{C}{d}$ column.

C Describe anything you notice about the ratio $\frac{C}{d}$ in your table.

_____

D The ratio of the circumference of a circle to its diameter is the same for all circles. The ratio is called **pi**, and its symbol is π.

So, for any circle, $\frac{C}{d} =$ _____.

As you discovered, the value of π is close to 3. A closer approximation is $\frac{22}{7}$, which in decimal form is about $\bigcirc.\bigcirc\bigcirc$.

E Write a formula for finding circumference C when given the diameter d.

$\dfrac{C}{\bigcirc} = \bigcirc$ Use the formula from Part D above.

$\dfrac{C}{d} \times \dfrac{d}{1} = \pi \times \dfrac{d}{1}$ Multiply both sides by d.

$C =$ _____   Simplify.

F Write a formula for finding circumference C when given the radius r.

$C =$ _____   Use the formula from Part E above.

$C = \pi \times 2 \times \bigcirc$ Substitute for d.   Remember, the diameter of a circle is twice its radius.

$C = 2\left(\bigcirc\right)$ Commutative Property

Reflect

1. **Make a Conjecture** How could you estimate the circumference of a circular object without measuring if you know its diameter?

_____

_____

2. **Communicate Mathematical Ideas** Are the formulas $C = \pi d$ and $C = 2\pi r$ equivalent? Explain.

_____

_____

_____

Finding the Circumference of a Circle

You can use the circumference formula to find the circumference C of a circle when you know the diameter d or the radius r.

EXAMPLE 1

Find the circumference of the circle to the nearest hundredth. Use 3.14 for π.

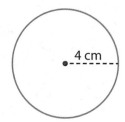

4 cm

The radius of the circle is 4 cm. Use the formula that includes the radius.

$C = 2\pi r$	*Write the formula.*
$C = 2 \times \pi \times 4$	*Substitute 4 for r.*
$C \approx 2(3.14)(4)$	*Substitute 3.14 for π.*
$C \approx 25.12$	*Multiply.*

Use $\approx$ because 3.14 is an approximation for π.

The circumference of the circle is about 25.12 centimeters.

Reflect

3. How do you know the answer is reasonable?

_____

_____

4. Analyze Relationships For what values of r would it be easier to use $\frac{22}{7}$ instead of 3.14 for *pi* when finding the circumference? Explain.

_____

_____

_____

5. Communicate Mathematical ideas How could you use $C = \pi d$ to find the circumference of the circle above?

_____

_____

Using Circumference

You can use the formulas for circumference to solve problems about real-world situations. Look at the given information to decide which circumference formula to use.

A remote-control drone is moving directly across the diameter of a circular field at a rate of 8 feet per second. The circumference of the field is 942 feet. How long does it take the drone to cross the field?

STEP 1 Sketch the field. Label what you know and what you need to find out.

STEP 2 Find the diameter of the field.

$$C = \underline{\hspace{1cm}}$$ *Use the formula that includes d.*

$$\underline{\hspace{1cm}} \approx \underline{\hspace{1cm}} d$$ *Substitute for the diameter and for π.*

$$\frac{942}{\boxed{}} \approx \frac{3.14d}{\boxed{}}$$ *Divide both sides by \underline{\hspace{2cm}}.*

$$\underline{\hspace{1cm}} \approx d$$ *Simplify.*

The diameter of the field is about \underline{\hspace{2cm}} feet.

STEP 3 Find the time it takes the drone to fly across the field.

Divide the diameter of the field by the drone's speed.

\underline{\hspace{2cm}} feet ÷ \underline{\hspace{2cm}} feet per second = \underline{\hspace{2cm}} seconds

It takes the drone about \underline{\hspace{2cm}} seconds to fly across the field.

Reflect

6. **What If?** How long would it take the drone to fly across the field if it traveled at a rate of 10 feet per second?

\underline{\hspace{15cm}}

\underline{\hspace{15cm}}

Finding the Perimeter of a Polygon

While the distance around a circle is its circumference, the distance around a polygon is its **perimeter**. To find the perimeter of a polygon, add the lengths of its sides.

> Just like circumference is the distance around a circle.

EXAMPLE 2

Find the perimeter to solve each problem.

A Mike is using strips of balsa wood to make a model of a bridge. The model will be built of equilateral triangles as shown. What length of balsa wood does he need for each triangle?

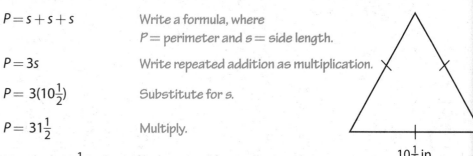

$P = s + s + s$	Write a formula, where $P =$ perimeter and $s =$ side length.
$P = 3s$	Write repeated addition as multiplication.
$P = 3(10\frac{1}{2})$	Substitute for s.
$P = 31\frac{1}{2}$	Multiply.

$10\frac{1}{2}$ in.

He needs $31\frac{1}{2}$ inches of balsa wood for each triangle.

B Jena made a garden in the shape of the rectangle shown. She makes a border of paving stones around it. How long is the border?

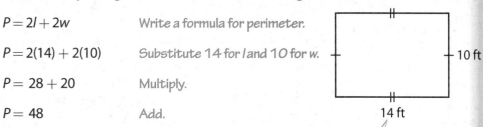

$P = 2l + 2w$	Write a formula for perimeter.
$P = 2(14) + 2(10)$	Substitute 14 for l and 10 for w.
$P = 28 + 20$	Multiply.
$P = 48$	Add.

10 ft

14 ft

The border of the garden is 48 feet long.

> Opposite sides of a rectangle are congruent, so it has two sides of length l and two sides of length w.

Practice

For 1–3, find the circumference of each circle to the nearest tenth. Tell whether you used 3.14 or $\frac{22}{7}$ for π.

1.

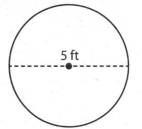

5 ft

_____

2.

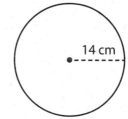

14 cm

_____

3.

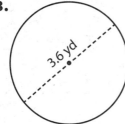

3.6 yd

_____

For 4–9, find the perimeter of each polygon.

4.

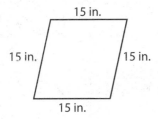

15 in.

15 in. 15 in.

15 in.

_____

5.

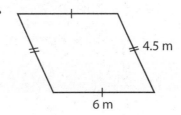

4.5 m

6 m

_____

6.

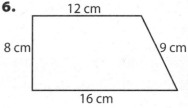

12 cm

8 cm 9 cm

16 cm

_____

7.

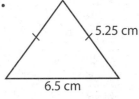

5.25 cm

6.5 cm

_____

8.

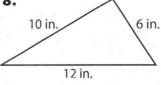

10 in. 6 in.

12 in.

_____

9.

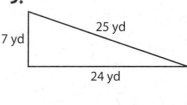

25 yd

7 yd

24 yd

_____

For 10–13, find each answer to the nearest tenth of a unit if necessary. Round π to 3.14.

10. A round cake pan has a circumference of 34.54 inches. What is the diameter of the cake pan?

_____

11. A circular pond has a diameter of 7 feet. How long will it take a ladybug moving 0.5 inch per second to walk all the way around the edge of the pond?

_____

12. A cafeteria table has a length of 6 feet and a width of 4 feet. Four tables are pushed together so their 4-foot ends touch.

  a. What is the perimeter of the larger table formed?

  _____

  b. Critique Reasoning A student says that pushing the tables together along the 6-foot length will give the same perimeter. Is the student correct? Explain.

  _____

  _____

13. A wooden tile is shaped like an isosceles triangle with a base of 4 centimeters and sides of 8 centimeters. A student pushes three of the tiles together to form a larger polygon. What is the perimeter of the polygon formed?

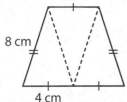

8 cm

4 cm

_____

LESSON
S.19 Area of Circles

? ESSENTIAL QUESTION

How do you find the area of a circle?

EXPLORE ACTIVITY

Exploring the Area of a Circle

You can use what you know about π and about the area of a parallelogram to find the formula for the area of a circle.

A Draw a large circle with a compass and then cut it out.
Fold the circle three times as shown to make eight equal wedges.

B Unfold the circle and shade one-half of it.
Cut the wedges apart and fit them together
to form a figure as shown.

C The figure looks somewhat like a parallelogram.
Its base and the height relate to the parts of a circle.

Base $b = \dfrac{\square}{\square}$ the circumference of the circle, or _____,

and the height $h =$ the _____ of the circle, or _____.

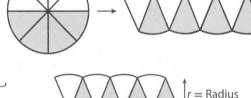

r = Radius
b = Half the circumference

D The formula for the area of a parallelogram is $A = bh$.
To find the area of a circle, substitute for b and h in the area formula.

$A = bh$

$A = \boxed{}h$ Substitute πr for b.

$A = \pi r\boxed{}$ Substitute r for h.

$A = \pi\boxed{}$ Use an exponent to write $r \times r$.

The formula for the area of a circle is $A =$ _____.

Reflect

1. **Make a Conjecture** What could you do to the circle to make a figure that looks more like a parallelogram?

_____

_____

Finding the Area of a Circle

The area of a circle is equal to π times the radius squared.

$$A = \pi r^2$$

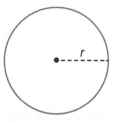

EXAMPLE 1

An artist makes circular clay pendants. Each circle has a radius of 2 centimeters. What is the area of a clay pendant? Use 3.14 for π.

$A = \pi r^2$	Write the formula.
$A = \pi \times 2^2$	Substitute 2 for r.
$\approx 3.14 \times 2^2$	Substitute 3.14 for π.
$= 3.14 \times 4$	Evaluate the power.
$= 12.56$	Multiply.

> Remember that area is always measured in square units.

The area of a clay pendant is about 12.56 square centimeters.

Reflect

1. **What If?** How would the answer differ if you use $\frac{22}{7}$ for π? Is either answer the exact value of the area? Explain.

_____

_____

_____

EXAMPLE 2

A cake platter has a circumference of 94.2 centimeters. What is the area of the platter?

STEP 1 Find the diameter of the platter.

$C = \pi d$	Write the formula for circumference.
$94.2 = \pi d$	Substitute 94.2 for C.
$94.2 \approx 3.14 \times d$	Substitute 3.14 for π.
$\dfrac{94.2}{3.14} \approx \dfrac{3.14 \times d}{3.14}$	Divide both sides of the equation by 3.14.
$30 \approx d$	Simplify.

The diameter of the platter is about 30 centimeters.

STEP 2 Find the radius.

$r = \frac{1}{2}d$ The radius is half of the diameter.

$r \approx \frac{1}{2}(30)$ Substitute 30 for d.

$r \approx 15$ Multiply.

The radius of the platter is about 15 centimeters.

STEP 3 Find the area.

$A = \pi r^2$ Write the area formula.

$A \approx 3.14 \times 15^2$ Substitute 3.14 for π and 15 for r.

$A \approx 3.14 \times 225$ Evaluate the power.

$A \approx 706.5$ Multiply.

The area of the cake platter is about 706.5 square centimeters.

Reflect

2. **What If?** Suppose you used $C = 2\pi r$ in Step 1.

   a. Would it change the final answer? Explain.

   _____

   b. Would it change the process? Explain.

   _____

   _____

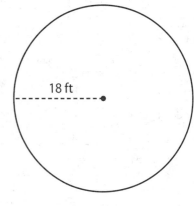

Practice

For 1–6, find the area of each circle to the nearest tenth. Use 3.14 for π.

1.

9 mm

2.

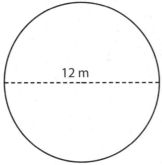

12 m

3.

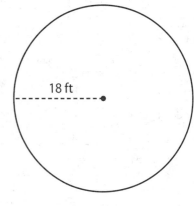

18 ft

_____   _____   _____

4.

5.2 in.

_____

5.

7.3 yd

_____

6.

6.25 cm

_____

For 7–10, find the answer to the nearest tenth. Use 3.14 for π.

7. The circular base of a pencil holder has a radius of 4 centimeters. What is the area of the base of the pencil holder?

_____

8. A circular rug has a circumference of 50.24 feet. What is the area of the rug?

_____

9. An irrigation system in Arizona waters circular areas of crops. If each circular field has a diameter of 60 feet, what is the area of each field?

_____

10. James took one slice out of the 14-inch pizza shown. What is the area of the slice of pizza?

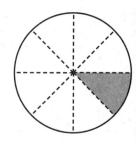

_____

11. Shaun is making a decorative walkway using concrete stepping stones that he will paint different colors. Each stepping stone has a radius of 0.5 foot.

a. What is the area of one stepping stone to the nearest tenth of a square foot?

_____

b. Shaun will paint 25 stepping stones. If one can of spray paint will cover 15 square feet, how many cans of spray paint does Shaun need to buy? Explain.

_____

_____

12. Critical Thinking The circular entrance to a small birdhouse has a circumference of 2π centimeters. The circular entrance to a larger birdhouse has a circumference of 4π centimeters. Is the area of the larger entrance twice the area of the smaller entrance? Explain your thinking.

_____

_____

_____

_____

LESSON S.20 Representing the Mean Graphically

ESSENTIAL QUESTION

How can you graphically represent the mean of a set of data?

EXPLORE ACTIVITY

Finding the Mean Using a Number Line

For after-school snacks, Kayden put crackers on four napkins. One friend said, "That's not fair!"

To find the fair share, Kayden moved one cracker at a time.

First she took a cracker from the share that had the most and moved it to the share that had the fewest.

The shares were still uneven, so she moved two more crackers.

Now all the shares are equal. The fair share amount is the *mean* of the original shares. You can also use a number line to find the fair share or mean.

A Begin by graphing points to represent the number of crackers in each portion.

```
   1  2  3  4  5  6  7  8  9  10
```

B The red arrow shows removing a cracker from the greatest number. The blue arrow shows adding that cracker to the least number.

> To keep the balance, when you decrease a value by one unit, you must increase a value by one unit.

Now two of the shares have 2 crackers, one has 3, and one has 5. Draw arrows to show removing a cracker from the share with 5. Then show adding a cracker to a share with 2.

C Now there is one share with ____ crackers, two shares with ____ crackers, and

one share with ____ crackers.

Draw arrows to show removing a cracker from the share at 4 and adding it to the share at 2. (Since there is already an arrow from 2 to 3, you can put the new arrow above it.)

D Combining the arrows shows the total change to each share.

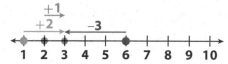

The total of the increases is _____ to the total decrease.

All of the shares ended up with ____ crackers, so that is the fair share.

E To check that the fair share is equal to the mean, calculate the mean of the numbers 1, 6, 2, and 3.

$$\frac{1 + \boxed{} + 2 + \boxed{}}{4} = \frac{\boxed{}}{4} = \boxed{}$$

Reflect

1. **Look for a Pattern** Count each one-unit arrow to the right as +1. Count each one-unit arrow to the left as −1. What is the sum of these numbers after finding the fair share? _____

Representing the Mean as the Balance Point

To find the mean of a data set on a number line, you can draw balanced arrows from each data point until all the arrows meet. The balance point, or the point where the arrows meet, is the mean.

EXAMPLE

Use a number line to find the mean as the balance point for each data set.

A 3, 11

(**STEP 1**) Graph each data point on the number line.

STEP 2 Draw arrows to show decreasing the greatest number and increasing the least number, one unit at a time.

> Make sure there is the same number of increases and decreases.

STEP 3 Combine the arrows to show the total increase and total decrease. Circle the value where the arrows meet. This is the balance point.

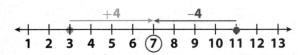

B 5, 10, 12

STEP 1 Graph each data point on the number line.

STEP 2 Draw equal-length arrows to show decreasing the greatest number and increasing the least number.

Stop when one of the arrows reaches one of the other data points, at 10.

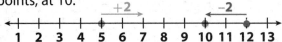

STEP 3 Add arrows to show decreasing both of the upper numbers.

Add an arrow increasing the lower number by a matching total amount.

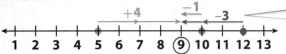

> The sum of the distances to the mean for all the points *above* the mean is the opposite of the sum of the distances for all the points *below* the mean.

Circle the value where the arrows meet.

The mean of the numbers 5, 10, and 12 is 9.

C 2, 2, 9, 11

STEP 1 Graph each data point on the number line.

STEP 2 Draw equal-length arrows from the two least data points and a balancing arrow from the greatest data point.

Stop when one of the arrows reaches one of the other data points, at 9.

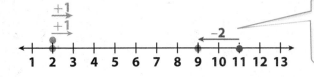

> When a data point is repeated, you can stack the graphed points on the number line.

STEP 3 Continue drawing balancing arrows from each data point.

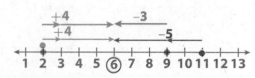

Check that the arrows balance: $4 + 4 = 8$; $-5 + (-3) = -8$.

Circle the value where the arrows meet.

The mean of the numbers 2, 2, 9, and 11 is 6.

Practice

1. The mean of a data set of three numbers is modeled on the number line.

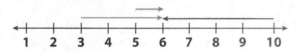

   a. What are the numbers in the data set?

   _____

   b. What is the mean?

   _____

   c. What is the total of the increases? The total of the decreases?

   _____

Use the number line to find the mean of each data set as the balance point.

2. 3, 4, 6, 8, 9 _____

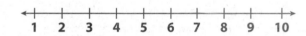

3. 1, 3, 8 _____

4. 1, 6, 6, 7 _____

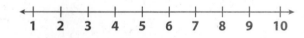

5. 3, 6, 9, 10 _____

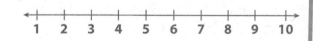

6. Aaron tracked his minutes of reading for 4 days: 21, 24, 27, 28.

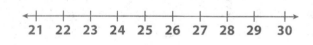

7. Six winners of the Nobel Peace Prize were in their thirties when they won. They won at these ages: 32, 32, 33, 35, 39, 39.

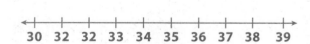

8. In the last three games, the basketball team scored 78, 81, and 75 points.

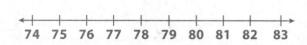

LESSON S.21 Mean, Median, and Outliers

? ESSENTIAL QUESTION

How much impact does removing a data point from a data set have on its mean and median?

EXPLORE ACTIVITY

Deleting or Inserting a Data Point

The dot plot shows a student's quiz scores during the year.

Quiz Scores

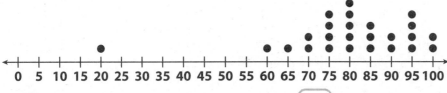

A Identify the quiz score that is an outlier. ☐

B Find the mean quiz score and median quiz score *with* the outlier.

STEP 1 To find the mean, find the sum of the data values and divide by the number of data values.

$$\frac{20 + 60 + 65 + 2(70) + 4(75) + 5(80) + 3(85) + 2(90) + 4(95) + 2(100)}{\boxed{}} = \frac{\boxed{}}{\boxed{}} = \boxed{}$$

STEP 2 To find the median, find the middle value. If there are two middle values, find the mean of the two values.

The median is $\boxed{}$.

C Find the mean quiz score and median quiz score *without* the outlier.

STEP 1 To find the mean *without* the outlier, remove the outlier value from the sum. Divide by the remaining number of data values.

$$\frac{\text{original sum} - \text{outlier value}}{\text{original number of data values} - 1} = \frac{\boxed{} - \boxed{}}{\boxed{} - 1} = \frac{\boxed{}}{\boxed{}} = \boxed{}$$

STEP 2 To find the median without the outlier, skip the first dot, then find the middle value. You may need to find the mean of two middle values.

The median is $\boxed{}$.

© Houghton Mifflin Harcourt Publishing Company

Lesson S.21 **SL81**

D Which measure was affected more by deleting the outlier?

(mean / median)

E Suppose the student takes another quiz, getting a score of 70. Find the mean and median of the original data *with* the added quiz score.

STEP 1 For the new mean, add the new value to the sum and divide by the new number of data values.

$$\frac{\text{original sum} + 70}{\text{original number of data values} + 1} = \frac{\boxed{}}{\boxed{}} \approx \boxed{}$$

STEP 2 To find the median, count the dots from left to right until you find the middle value. You may need to find the mean of two middle values.

The median is $\boxed{}$.

Reflect

1. **Analyze Relationships** How does removing a data value impact the mean and the median? Explain.

_____

_____

_____

_____

Finding Measures of Center Using Technology

EXAMPLE

Use a spreadsheet and a graphing calculator to create a dot plot and a box plot for the quiz data in the Explore Activity. Identify the measures of center that can be read from the plots.

A Create a dot plot.

STEP 1 Represent each score by an ordered pair in which *x* is the score and *y* is a count of each occurrence of the score.

Enter each ordered pair in columns A and B of a spreadsheet as shown.

	A	B
1	20	1
2	60	1
3	65	1
4	70	1
5	70	2
6	75	1
7	75	2
8	75	3
9	75	4
...	...	...
24	100	1
25	100	2

Since
are 2
of 7(
wa
dots
(70,
(70,

STEP 2 Select both columns A and B as shown in **STEP 1**. From the Chart tab, select Scatter, then Marked Scatter to create a scatter plot of the ordered pairs.

The scatter plot should match the dot plot shown in the Explore Activity.

STEP 3 From a dot plot, you can find the median and mode. The mean and range can be calculated.

B Create a box plot.

STEP 1 Enter each score into list L1 of a graphing calculator.

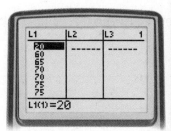

STEP 2 Select the box plot option from the STAT PLOT menu, then select ZoomStat from the ZOOM menu to create the box plot.

 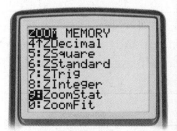

STEP 3 Use ⎣Trace⎦ and the arrow keys to see the 5 key measures from left to right.

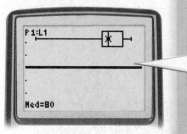

Min = 20
Q1 = 75
Med = 80
Q3 = 92.5
Max = 100

From a box plot, you can find the median but cannot determine the mean.

STEP 4 From a box plot, you can find the median. The range can be calculated.

Reflect

2. **What If?** Suppose you need to create a representation of data where the mean can be found. Which data display should you choose? Explain.

For 1–3, use the data set 1, 7, 1, 3, 3, 9, 5, 8, 37, 3, 4, 2, 10, 6, 6.

1. Make a box plot of the data. Find the mean and median.

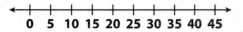

_____

2. Make a dot plot of the data without the outlier. Find the new mean and median.

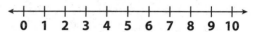

_____

3. Which measure of center was *least* affected by removing the outlier? Explain.

_____

_____

4. The Fibonacci sequence is 1, 1, 2, 3, 5, 8, 13, 21, 34, 55, …, where each term is the sum of the previous two terms.

  a. Find the mean and median of the terms given above.

    _____

  b. Find the next term, and then find the new mean and median. How much does the mean increase? How much does the median increase? Round to the nearest tenth.

    _____

    _____

5. Katie collects starfish. All the starfish she has collected so far have 5 arms. She finds one with fewer arms and adds it to her collection. Describe the new mean and median number of arms on the starfish.

_____

6. **Critical Thinking** For a data set containing only one value, both the mean and median are equal to that value. What is the smallest number of data values needed for the mean and median of a data set to differ? Explain.

_____

_____

_____

_____

? **ESSENTIAL QUESTION**

How can you represent data using a circle graph?

Interpreting Circle Graphs

A **circle graph** shows each category of data compared to the whole.

A circle graph is divided into **sectors**, each of which represents part of the data set. Sectors are often labeled as a percent of the whole data set.

Circle graphs are easier to use when there are few categories; too many will make it difficult to read.

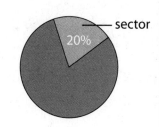

sector

20%

EXPLORE ACTIVITY 1

Twenty-five football players were chosen for the All-County team. The circle graph below shows the districts they represent.

A What categories are shown on the graph?

_____

_____

B One sector is missing its percent label.
What is the sum of the known percents? _____
What percent is missing, and what category does this represent?

_____

All-County Players by District

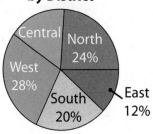

Central North 24%

West 28%

South 20%

East 12%

C How many players are from the West District?

$$\frac{\cdot p}{25} = \frac{\boxed{}}{100}$$

> What number is 100 divided by to equal 25? Divide numerator by the same dividend to find p.

$p =$ _____ players

D How many players are from the East District? _____

E There are _____ players from the east and _____ players from the west, so there are _____ more players from the west than from the east.

F How many players are there from the east and west combined? _____
What percent of players are from the east and west combined? _____

Reflect

1. **Critical Thinking** How many categories do you think would make a circle graph too difficult to read? How could you reduce the number of categories?

_____

_____

EXPLORE ACTIVITY 2

Creating Circle Graphs

The school pet club voted for club mascot. A circle graph can show the results of the vote.

Follow the instructions in Parts A and B to complete the table. Then shade and label the circle as described in Part C to make a circle graph.

A Find the ratio of votes for each mascot to the total number of votes.

The total number of votes is $\boxed{}$.

$$\frac{\text{votes for pug as mascot}}{\text{total votes}} = \frac{8}{\boxed{}}$$

Repeat the calculation for the other mascots to complete the **Ratio of Votes to Total Votes** column of the table.

Mascot	Votes	Ratio of Votes to Total Votes	Percent
Pug	8		
Parrot	2		
Iguana	6		
Ferret	4		
Total		$\frac{20}{20}$	**100%**

B Find the percent of the circle needed for each mascot.

$$\frac{\text{votes for pug as mascot}}{\text{total votes}} = \frac{\text{percent for pug}}{100}$$

$$\times\boxed{}$$

$$\frac{8}{\boxed{}} = \frac{\boxed{}}{100} = \boxed{}\%$$

$$\times\boxed{}$$

What number do you need to multiply the numerator and denominator by in order to make an equivalent ratio?

Repeat the calculation for the other mascots to complete the **Percent** column of the table.

C Complete the circle graph using the steps below.

Title: _____

> Begin at "12 o'clock" and move clockwise to shade each new sector.

STEP 1 The circle shown has ⬭ sectors (slices). Use an equivalent ratio to find the number of sectors to shade for each mascot.

$$\frac{\text{percent for pug}}{100} = \frac{\text{number of sectors for pug}}{\text{total sectors}}$$

$\dfrac{\Box}{100} = \dfrac{\Box}{\Box} \longrightarrow$ Shade ⬭ of the ⬭ sectors for pug.

Repeat the calculation for the other mascots.

STEP 2 Begin at the top of the circle and move clockwise. Use a different color for each mascot, and shade the correct number of sectors for each.

STEP 3 Give the graph a title. Label each sector to show which mascot it represents.

Reflect

2. What percent of the votes were for either parrot or ferret? _____

3. **What If?** Suppose one vote for "iguana" was not counted. How would the circle graph change if that vote were added? Explain.

_____

_____

_____

_____

_____

1. Clarissa surveyed students and asked them to pick their favorite team. She made a circle graph of the data.

   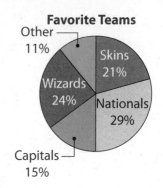
   Favorite Teams
   Other 11%
   Skins 21%
   Wizards 24%
   Nationals 29%
   Capitals 15%

   a. What team got the greatest number of votes?

   _____

   b. What team got about $\frac{1}{4}$ of the votes?

   _____

A survey of 50 students asked each one to name a favorite free-time activity. The results are shown in the circle graph. For 2–5, use the graph.

2. What percent of students chose "Other"? How many students does this represent?

   _____

   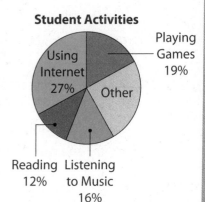
   Student Activities
   Playing Games 19%
   Using Internet 27%
   Other
   Reading 12%
   Listening to Music 16%

3. Which is the most popular activity?

   _____

4. Which activity was chosen by 6 students?

   _____

5. The survey results listed 9 different activities. Was Reading the least popular activity? Justify your reasoning.

   _____

   _____

   _____

6. The math grades for Ms. Jackson's 6th grade students are shown in the table. Make a circle graph of the data. Sketch your graph on the circle, and label each sector with the category and percent. Remember to include a title.

   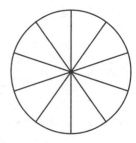

Grade	A	B	C	D
Number of Students	16	12	8	8

LESSON S.23 Comparing Data Represented in Graphs

? ESSENTIAL QUESTION

How does data represented in a circle graph appear different than the same data represented in a bar graph, pictograph, or line plot?

EXPLORE ACTIVITY 1

Comparing a Circle Graph with a Pictograph

Pictographs are used to show and compare data about items that can be grouped into categories.

The circle graph and pictograph both show the estimated number of giraffes in five countries. Use the graphs to answer the questions below.

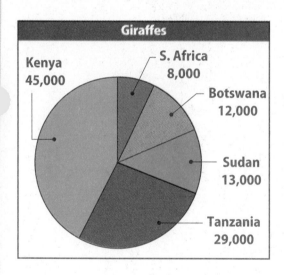

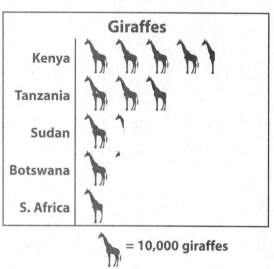

= 10,000 giraffes

A _____ has the most giraffes with _____ giraffes.

_____ has the fewest giraffes with _____ giraffes.

B Which country has the second-most giraffes?_____

Kenya has _____ more giraffes than Tanzania.

C In which graph is it easier to see this information? Explain.

_____

_____

Comparing a Circle Graph With a Bar Graph

Bar graphs are used to show data that can be grouped into categories, such as the amount of rain each month or the number of people with each eye color. You can use a bar graph to make comparisons between different groups.

Compare these graphs of a store's sales of running shoes during one week.

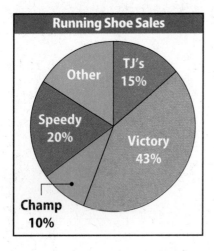

A The store manager wants to know what percent of sales were "Other."

How can you find the answer using the circle graph?

_____

How can you find the answer using the bar graph?

_____

What percent of sales were "Other"? _____.

B How might the circle graph be useful to the store manager?

_____

_____

C How might the bar graph be useful to the store manager?

_____

_____

Reflect

1. **Communicate Mathematical Ideas** What information can you find in each graph that is not in the other?

_____

_____

Comparing a Circle Graph with a Dot Plot

Dot plots, also called line plots, are used to show frequency for numerical data.

In the dot plot below, each dot represents one quiz with the score shown on the number line below it.

EXAMPLE

Compare the circle graph and dot plot showing Monique's quiz scores.

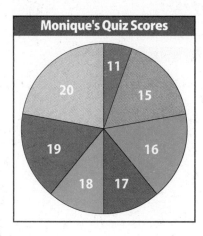

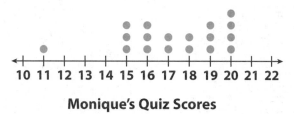

Monique's Quiz Scores

A   Is there an outlier? Which graph shows this more clearly?

Yes; Monique had only one score of 11, and no other scores close to it, so it is an outlier. The dot plot shows this clearly.

> The circle graph shows the same score of 11, but it is not as obvious how far that score is from the others.

B   Which graph gives a better picture of Monique's overall performance on the quizzes? In what way?

The dot plot. You can see that she scored at least 15 on all but one quiz, that her quiz scores were about evenly spread between 15 and 20, and that she got a 20 more often than any other score.

C   Which graph would be better for finding her average quiz score? Why?

The dot plot. You know the number of quizzes she took because there are 18 dots. You can directly average her scores. The circle graph does not show the number of quizzes, so it is harder to calculate her average.

D   Monique scored 18 or higher on half of her quizzes. On which graph can you see this without counting? Explain.

The circle graph. The three sectors on the left of the graph represent scores of 18, 19, and 20, and they make up half of the graph.

Practice

Determine the type of graph you would use to display the data below.

1. The number of times a baseball player batted:

Year	2017	2018	2019	2020
At Bats	275	504	478	496

_____

2. The number of siblings students have:

Number of Siblings	0	1	2	3	4 or more
Students	8	10	11	4	3

_____

A group of students were surveyed and asked to name their favorite pet. For 3-4, use the graphs below.

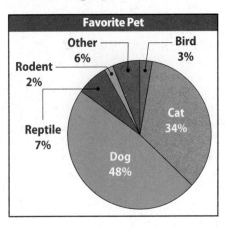
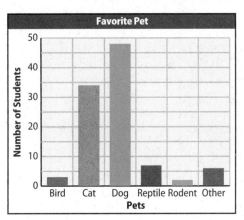

3. What information about the students' favorite pets can be found using only the circle graph?

_____

4. What information from the table *cannot* be found using only the circle graph?

_____

Mr. Jackson asked his students how they usually get to school. For 5–6, use the graphs below.

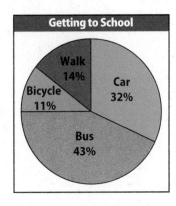
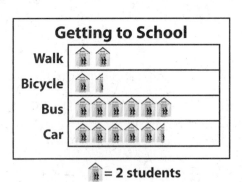

5. Which graph is better for finding the number of students who ride the bus?

_____

6. Which graph is better for estimating the fraction of students who go to school by car?

_____